# CONCILIUM

*Religion in the E*

# CONCILIUM

*Concilium* 144 (4/1981): Practical Theology

# TENSIONS
# BETWEEN
# THE CHURCHES
# OF THE FIRST WORLD
# AND THE
# THIRD WORLD

Edited by

**Virgil Elizondo**

and

**Norbert Greinacher**

English Language Editor
**Marcus Lefébure**

**T. & T. CLARK LTD.**
Edinburgh

**THE SEABURY PRESS**
New York

April 1981
T. & T. Clark Ltd., 36 George Street, Edinburgh EH2 2LQ
ISBN: 0 567 30024 2

The Seabury Press, 815 Second Avenue, New York, N.Y. 10017
ISBN: 0 8164 2311 3

Library of Congress Catalog Card No.: 80 54386

Printed in Scotland by William Blackwood & Sons Ltd., Edinburgh

*Concilium:* Monthly except July and August.
Subscriptions 1981: All countries (except U.S.A. and Canada) £27·00 postage and handling included; U.S.A. and Canada $64.00 postage and handling included. (Second class postage licence 541-530 at New York, N.Y.) Subscription distribution in U.S. by Expediters of the Printed Word Ltd., 527 Madison Avenue, Suite 1217, New York, N.Y. 10022.

# CONTENTS

# Part III

# Part IV
# Bulletin

# Editorial:
# Do We Really Have
# Third World Churches?

PREVIOUS ISSUES of *Concilium* have presented various aspects of a new pluralism arising within the life and understanding of Christianity. While this pluralism is not even suspected or desired by some segments of the Church, it is a reality of life for many others. This issue of practical theology will explore some of the tensions which arise out of the actual expressions of this pluralism.

We are all aware of the many and different uses of the term 'First World' and 'Third World'. For the sake of this issue, we are taking western Europe and North America as the First World. We are taking 'Third World' to include those regions of the world where the poor, marginated, and the disinherited of the earth constitute the great masses of the populations. They are also the ones who were missionised, conquered and colonised by western European powers. The conquest imposed a new social order, a new religion and even a new world vision. Even though there has been political independence for many of these peoples, in many ways they still continue to be economically and culturally dominated and in general dependent peoples.

The more one sees the totality of today's situation the more one is forced to ask: do we really have Third World churches in the full theological sense of the term 'church'? It seems that the process of generating new churches generally came to an end with the close of the first millenium. Since then the churches of the Old World went out to impose their ecclesiological models upon the rest of the world.

The world situation is such that the emergence and development of new churches will not be easy. It is evident that they do not have their own financial base, intellectual formation, catechetics, liturgy, church law and personnel. Many of these churches are still dependent on foreign episcopacy, personnel, finances and formation. The West still appears to be the centre of all power and authority. All truth still appears to be coming out of the western universities and mediated through the ways of western civilisation.

Nevertheless, given the power of God's word to triumph beyond our own human endeavours, the seeds of the gospel were deeply planted. They have been gradually taking root and today we find the beginning of the flourishing of truly new churches of the Third World on the peripheries of the churches of the Old World.

Out of the suffering and misery of the churches of the Third World the Spirit is bringing about a newness which will truly purify, enrich and bring new life to the enslaving and dying forms of the churches of the Old World. This evangelising newness is not coming out of the great universities or centres of power. It is emerging spontaneously and throughout the churches of the Third World out of the response of the people to God's word. It emerges in the many grass-roots movements such as the *Comunidades de Base* and the multiple groups of people who gather around the ministers of the Word to hear God's message and to seek to respond to it in faith. The believing people become aware that they are the Church and that the Church is theirs, for the gospel is addressed perpetually to the poor and in their response to it, begin the kingdom for all others.

There is a real revival of the Christianity of the gospels and of the apostolic era in many segments of the Third World.

As no one ever expected anything of value to come out of Galilee, certainly none of the intelligent and educated according to the wisdom of this world had expected anything to come out of the so-called 'backward' and 'underdeveloped' countries and peoples of the world. Yet, it is precisely here that we discover a new ecclesiological freshness which had been totally unsuspected and unimagined. The Church of the third millenium is beginning to take shape among the poor people of today's Third World.

This birth and coming of age of the new churches of the world are bringing about some unexpected tensions within the communion of the churches. However, these tensions are not unhealthy or destructive. On the contrary, they are signs of life. As Morgan points out in his article, the examples of Jesus and Paul suggest that the richness, power and attraction of the gospel is revealed through theological tensions rather than by eliminating them. It is the conviction of the authors of this issue that these tensions far from being destructive of the fundamental catholicity and unity of the Church will facilitate the emergence of new and more resplendent expressions of the true unity and universality of the one Church. They are the most precious gift of the Spirit in our times. They will purify the universal Church of its western-centred enslavement. This purification will lead to a deeper unity and a more evident universality. Our Catholic unity cannot be the unity of imposition, which is the unity of this world which seeks to dominate. The unity of the gospel gives new birth to new churches each characterised by its own language, heritage, music, art, wisdom, reflection and liturgical expression. It is the Spirit which turns this diversity into the constructive elements of a new humanity. The Church takes nothing away from what God has been cultivating through the creativity of each particular people (LG § 17).

It opens people up to a new universality of human communion and participation based on the experience of the common fatherhood of God, but it does not destroy the originality and the unique charisms of the people.

After an initial study and consultation of the various issues involved in this question, we have decided to divide this edition into three parts: (I) the conflictual reality of the churches in the midst of today's multiply divided world; (II) some theological insights into the historical development of the tensions of unity and pluralism; and finally, (III) some concrete expressions of the new forms of church life which are emerging and pose a challenge to the present ecclesial order which still tends to see unity as uniformity.

Because the Church exists in the world and cannot operate or even think independently of it, we have started our issue with Houtart's analysis of the world situation of inequality and global oppression. It is devastating! By analysing some documents of the national hierarchies, Füssel brings out how different ecclesiologies develop out of the different social economic conditions. Since the theologians are not immune from this conditioning, Chenu exposes clearly how they too are in need of liberation. He brings out how the theological activity of the Third World is neither an imitation nor a development but the birth of new forms of theologising which will be liberating of all theologians everywhere.

In part two we have turned to the tradition of the Church for illumination. Morgan states the clear-cut affirmation of the New Testament: unity that respects diversity is a Christian ideal which will never be easy, but must always be struggled for. Cunningham states how the very quest for unity in essentials led the post-apostolic churches to a great wealth of diversity. In her telescopic article, Folliard presents how the efforts to help the masses become a people developed the ideal of a church and an empire united together as Christendom. This model would project uniformity as the basis for unity. Dussel develops the consequences of this empire—church unity in a missionary expansion of the Church beginning in the fourteenth century. The Church and the ways of Europe were imposed on new peoples, but new churches were not allowed to emerge.

Finally in part three, we have presented some of the very concrete and hopeful signs of new life that are taking place in churches throughout the world. We have started with the most basic—the experience of Church at the grass-roots. C. Boff of Brazil presents the uniqueness, dynamism and power of the *Comunidades Ecclesiales de Base*. Not only is a new ecclesiology emerging but likewise a new concept of theologian. The *comunidades* are the 'collective theologians' where no one theologises for anyone. The theologian *per se* is the believing community seeking to clarify and develop the meaning of its faith. This does not eliminate the need for specialists, but it does situate them in the midst of the suffering, the struggles and the joys of the people. This demands new standards of accreditation and credibility of theologians. No longer are degrees, teaching positions and publications the ultimate criteria, but communion and participation in the common life and struggles of the people. As Gustavo Gutiérrez has often pointed out, theology can no longer be done as work during the day, but it must now be done as reflection at the end of the working day. Van Nieuwenhove brings out the implications of Puebla for the Universal Church. It is the Church of the poor which puts in question the entire Church. Will the churches of the centre which are accustomed to being the teachers be able to become learners? Or even equal partners in the dialogue? Cardinal Arns of São Paulo, Brazil, brings the issue to a close with a challenging and futuristic article on how to translate the theological catholicity of the Church into a sociological reality. This will not come through the new theories or theologies but through the concrete living out of the churches' option for the poor. It is through the fellowship of charity that the full catholicity of the churches will emerge in the fullness of its splendour.

VIRGIL ELIZONDO
NORBERT GREINACHER

# PART I

*The Conflictual Reality of the Churches*

François Houtart

# The Global Aspects of Dependence and Oppression

THERE IS no getting away from the fact that at the beginning of the United Nations Third Development Decade (1980-1990) neither the results of the first two decades nor the prospects for the forthcoming one are very encouraging. Almost everywhere there is disappointment, caused by the fact that the gap between the North and the South, far from having been closed, has grown.[1] On a closer look there is nothing surprising about such a situation. All the factors involved seem such as to make it impossible to be otherwise, and only bad analyses, deliberate or not, could lead to other conclusions. This is a very important circumstance for any moral judgment which seeks to go beyond a denunciation of effects and get to grips with causes.

Thus twenty years ago in Latin America, a number of episcopates were describing dramatic social situations, in the north-east of Brazil, in Chile and in Colombia. At the beginning of 1980 CEPAL (the United Nations Economic Commission for Latin America) published figures indicating that in these very countries the structure of land distribution remained the same, that the number of children dying before the age of five had risen considerably in Colombia and Argentina, that, for example, malnutrition in Brazil was causing widespread mental retardation in children. In short, few fundamental changes—and those there have been in the direction of increased repression. Speeches by religious leaders, when they refer to these situations, remain much the same, that is on the one hand descriptive and on the other moralistic, without any connecting analysis either of causes or of the social dynamic of the relations between oppressors and oppressed. So in twenty or forty years' time, will we still find the same situations and the same speeches—unless, as in Nicaragua or El Salvador, the forces of revolution have changed both?

This article will first summarise some aspects of economic oppression, in particular technological dependence. It will then discuss the social and cultural consequences.

### 1. THE ECONOMIC FOUNDATIONS OF OPPRESSION

Since the traditional mechanisms for producing economic dependence are familiar, we need do no more than mention one or two of them. The principal one is the transfers of wealth from the South to the North as a result of the imbalance in the sale of primary

3

products and manufactured goods. The prices of raw materials or agricultural products are fixed by the interests of the purchaser, while those of manufactured goods have constantly risen at the same rate as the cost of living in western countries. In the last twenty years the switch of certain types of production to regions where labour is cheap has done no more than add a further cause of dependence and oppression, since the bulk of the surplus value produced has gone abroad while the type of economic activity concerned has increased the weight of foreign debt and accelerated inflation. Brazil is a good example. In 1980 the cost of servicing the foreign debt rose to $7,000 million and inflation was running at an annual rate of 96 per cent. Needless to say, earnings did not rise at the same pace. Transfers of production are mainly brought about by the activities of transnational companies. It was estimated that even in 1966 a third of the total manufactured production of Third World countries came from these companies.[2]

An important part of the conventional solution for the problems of the Third World is development aid. In fact, in its present structure, this aid tends above all to reinforce phenomena of dependence. According to figures from the early 1970s, at least 75 per cent of bilateral aid was tied to purchases in the donor country. This was true of two-thirds of British aid, and 80 per cent of aid from Japan and West Germany, and 93 per cent of the funds of the United States Agency for International Development (AID) were spent in the USA.

This also creates technological dependence on material and personnel which often lasts much longer than officially planned and forces Third World countries to agree to totally useless and even harmful expenditure. This can be illustrated by two examples from Zaïre.[3] Belgium financed the infrastructure of a new airport at Kisangani, a medium-sized town of 250,000 people with an airport whose runway had recently been renewed and could take Boeing 737s and DC9s. Belgium provided 500 million Belgian francs ($18 million) of financing on condition that the work should be given to a Belgian firm. The new runway is the longest in Central Africa, 4 kilometres long by 200 metres wide. The installations are luxurious. Zaïre made a matching investment of $40 million for the completion of the work, a sum which represented the total annual income of the region served by the airport. Belgian private companies made appreciable profits and the institutionalisation of dependence was reinforced.

The other case, cited by the same author, is that of 'Voice of Zaïre City', a complex of buildings situated on 12 hectares in the centre of Kinshasa and designed to house radio and television. A group of French companies carried out the work. The French government made a loan of 65 million francs, granted aid of 10 million francs and guaranteed credit amounting to 228 million francs. However, Zaïre had to make an equivalent contribution, i.e., about $75 million. There was also a contract for a plan for technical support and training which was to cost Zaïre 60 million francs, plus after-sales service. A year after completion the complex was still not in use for lack of competent personnel, and a partial start of operations was made possible only by the subsequent arrival of 150 French technicians.

One of the results of this type of aid is illustrated by Zaïre's foreign debt of $3,200 million, and in particular by the fact that the standard of living of urban workers went from an index of 100 in 1960 to 20 in 1977 as a result of inflation.[4]

The big international financial bodies are also very little understood by the public. They are often thought of as institutions of the international community designed to finance the economic development of Third World countries. Paul VI's gift of a million dollars to Latin America after his journey to Bogotá was accordingly channelled through the Inter-American Development Bank. In fact, the activity of bodies such as the International Monetary Fund and its regional equivalents is designed primarily to encourage a capitalist type of economic growth, which in the end simply makes the situation worse. For example the large-scale construction financed by the World Bank in the Philippines encourages the implantation of multinationals in the country. This is true of the dams designed to provide electricity, and the improvements to the port of Manila (the famous Tondo area) are intended to facilitate access by Japanese vessels which have already accelerated the collapse of the local fishing industry. In Sri Lanka international financial aid, organised chiefly by the International Monetary Fund, was subject to a devaluation of the rupee and the opening of the domestic market to foreign products, which increased the foreign debt. The result has been an increased level of consumption, but at the same time much greater social inequality than before.

We shall now examine more closely some of the effects, first of industrial and then of agricultural dependence. Industrial independence is in fact very slight in the Third World. One simple statistic will give an idea: seven Third World countries account for 70 per cent of the production of manufactured goods, while that of all the rest makes up only 30 per cent. These seven include Brazil, Mexico, India, South Korea and Taiwan, and the type of industrialisation concerned in most of these cases is well known. According to World Bank figures, the western countries in 1975 accounted for 80·9 per cent of the manufactured products exported in the world, the socialist countries for 9·5 per cent and all the developing countries another 9·5 per cent. The share of the developing countries was 5·7 per cent in 1960, and is expected to be 15·6 per cent in 1990.[5] Unfortunately almost the whole of this increase is due to the implantation of transnational companies.

To take an even more vivid example, in Argentina a study carried out in 1977 showed that almost half the 120 main industries of the country are controlled by foreign capital. Fifty-four out of 120 are foreign and they are situated in the three main sectors of industrial production, the food industry, the metal industry and the chemical industry, representing on their own almost 68 per cent of the national industrial product.[6]

In 1979 the European Economic Community was in the process of renewing the Lomé Convention, which deals with economic relations with ACP (Africa, Carribean and Pacific) countries, that is fifty-six former colonies of the Nine. The World Confederation of Labour organised a conference on the issue in Geneva.[7] It commented first that the EEC sold much more to the ACP countries than it bought from them. Nevertheless the supply of primary products and agricultural products is still a very important economic function of the ACP countries in relation to Europe. The EEC was also asking for guarantees for private investment, though there was no corresponding guarantee for workers or for the development of local food crops. There is no provision for facilitating trade between the ACP states or for developing their own energy sources. In short, the Confederation concludes, 'Lomé II is marked by the type of industrial redeployment and opening of markets which is conceived by and for "market forces". In plain terms this means ensuring Europe's security in the supply of primary products, increasing sales of "made in Europe" products in ACP countries and transferring certain non-profitable sectors to the Third World.'[8]

The industrial take-off of the developing countries is thus largely subordinate to the interests of the developed countries or, to be more precise, of the economic powers localised in those countries and the social classes which control them. But no situation can be analysed as if it were static. Each contains its own contradictions and therefore a dynamic which is not always intended. Thus the massive investments in South Korea, first from America and Japan and later from West Germany, France, Britain and Italy, have finally produced a local working class and the beginnings of a capitalist bourgeoisie. The latter functioned first as an intermediary but later accumulated a capital of its own. Foreign investments were attracted by low wages and the political stability guaranteed by the combination of military dictatorship and the American presence. Now that, as a result of pressure from the workers (despite the ban on trade unions) wages have been forced to rise, foreign firms are tending to disinvest and move elsewhere, and some Korean capital is also beginning to follow a similar course.

All these reasons illustrate how this model of relationship in the industrial sector essentially benefits the developed countries. According to figures for 1970, investment originating in America reached $270 million in Africa and repatriated profits had risen to $996 million. For Asia the figures were $200 million and $2,400 million, for Latin America $900 million and $2,900 million. It was estimated at the same time that secretly repatriated profits from this continent probably reached a total equal to the official profits.

But it is not just industry. Today agriculture is increasingly becoming an area for speculation as certain regions lack food and certain crops can be transformed into alcohol suitable for use as automobile fuel. This has a particular effect on Third World countries. The FAO estimates that the cereal deficit of these countries will reach 60-100 million tonnes in 1985.[9] One reason for this is the extension of what are called commercial crops at the expense of food crops, that is of production for export at the expense of local consumption. Nor is this the only imbalance. The developed countries annually consume 58·3 kg. of fertiliser per inhabitant, while the developing countries consume 6·7 kg. (1975 figures).[10] Part of this fertiliser is produced in developing countries. With the increase in population, the needs of Third World countries increase at the same time as their vulnerability. In addition the development of a minority of the population which this model favours simply increases imports of a wider range of foodstuffs as the needs of this class are modelled on the consumption of the affluent classes of the western countries.

All this reinforces food dependence, reflected practically in special ties with the United States. The USA accounts for 45 per cent of world grain exports, 60 per cent of cereals for animal food, 25 per cent of rice and 83 per cent of soya beans.[11] Agricultural exports represent between a fifth and a quarter of all American exports.[12] In 1978 their value was calculated at $27,000 million. Current world developments are tending to place the United States in a more strongly monopolistic position, which enables it both to influence prices and to use food as a weapon. The second aspect has a double function. The first is commercial. 'The big markets of the future,' Senator McGovern stated, 'are precisely the regions where vast sectors of the population are learning, through the "Food for Peace" programme, to eat American food. Those whom we aid today will be our customers tomorrow.'[13]

The second function is political. The same programme (PL 480) provided Chile after the 1973 coup with food to a value of $57·7 million, while all the other Latin American countries received no more than $9 million worth of aid in the same year.[14]

It is, of course, not difficult to understand the economic consequences of these features of domination or their political and sometimes military effects. However, there are other aspects deserving of special attention and the first of these also belongs to the economic sphere. This is technological dependence. Western technology is being introduced into countries which have not produced it. This would not be harmful in itself were this process not marked by two fundamental characteristics, first an unshakable sense of its superiority and second its commercial character. The former generally leads to the sheer destruction of old technologies, which could have been integrated into a more harmonious development, in the way that China and Vietnam have integrated traditional and modern medicine. But this is not all. Techno-economic logic is also a form of ideology which brings with it a whole conception of life, a way of occupying space, envisaging communications, using available raw materials, etc. The 'missionaries' of technology are often not aware of this aspect of things and set off mechanisms which destroy ways of life and cultural values with no process of transition and no social adaptation.[15]

The second characteristic is even more serious. Technology is not transmitted in a vacuum, and while the level of technology rises dependence on its sources also increases. A vicious circle is created, because the introduction of one element of technology often brings another in its train. The monopoly of patents also makes the technology market totally opaque and it is all too typical that at the Vienna Conference organised by the United Nations in 1979 (United Nations Conference for Science and Technology at the Service of Development) no concession was made by the developed countries in this area, despite the demands of the developing countries. It is increasingly the transnational companies which possess technological control. This is yet another element on top of the direct commercial relations which makes developing countries even more dependent. Not even the introduction of what is today called 'appropriate technology', though based on a sound intuition, completely escapes from this.

A further aspect is the fact that techniques give rise to particular forms of organisation and new rôles. For example, in a study published in 1974, the World Bank showed that it was possible to condition palm oil in such a way as to increase the income of peasants by 50 per cent and reduce investment costs by 70 per cent in comparison with a centralised western-type development project.[16] The multiplication of rôles results in the formation of a group of technocrats who often have little awareness of the social and political dimensions of their work. In commerce between socialist countries, too, similar phenomena can be noted, especially as regards the cultural aspects of technology, which sometimes produce very marked dependence effects, together with waste and imbalance. Here, however, while commercial considerations are not totally absent, they are not the final arbiters as in capitalist countries.

## 2. THE SOCIAL CONSEQUENCES OF ECONOMIC ORGANISATION

We have already mentioned several social consequences, but two of them deserve detailed consideration. The first consists in the unplanned, and therefore abrupt, decline of traditional structures. Firstly, small local industries are often eliminated by competition. In Kenya, for example, the arrival of the soap multinationals destroyed a local manufacturing process which employed a lot of labour and less advanced technology. The dietary effects of the introduction of industrial crops are often catastrophic.[17] This has been the case in several Latin American countries. In Mexico foreign companies which install this sort of cultivation in areas formerly cultivated by Indians or mestizo peasants have brought about a decline in the production of maize, the traditional food. Imports of wheat from the United States increase every year, but the peasants have not a high enough income to buy it. Their undernourishment is increasing even as agricultural income rises. In Peru, when the American firm Carnation started operations in the district of Arequipa, it destroyed the small-scale production of butter and cheese. In this way a type of popular consumption disappeared to the advantage of the affluent classes of the cities.[18] This phenomenon has been reported many times in connection with the activities of Nestlé too.

Still in the same sector, jobs have been destroyed rather than new jobs being created. The 'green revolution' in India produced considerable losses. It is estimated that in ten years two-thirds of women had been driven out of agricultural production, a fall from 27 million to 9 million. The number of landless peasants almost doubled. Similar phenomena are reported from Latin America. In 1972 it was estimated that over 2 million rural jobs had been eliminated. What makes this serious is that such jobs are not replaced by the creation of industrial jobs. Investment by transnationals, contrary to what is sometimes thought—and above all contrary to the justification offered by local governments—does not create employment on a large scale. What is transferred is routine, mechanised production. This has the advantage of not developing too large a

B

working class or developing one too fast. This economic policy, associated with political régimes which reduce social and political rights, makes possible a rapid accumulation of capital, which is necessary in the present phase of capitalism as it faces world-wide concentration on the one hand and a relative decline of rates of accumulation in certain sectors of central capitalism on the other. This is thus being paid for by the class of the workers of the Third World, though at least part of the unemployment in the countries of Europe and North America is also caused by transfers of production to low-wage areas.

The pressure on real wages in the Third World is also considerable. We have already quoted the case of Zaïre, but the phenomenon is general. In India it is estimated that between 1961 and 1977 the real earnings of a worker in manufacturing industry fell by a third,[19] and it should not be forgotten that over 40 per cent of the total population (especially in the country) lives below the 'poverty line', i.e., the minimum for survival, and that the bottom 20 per cent have seen their situation deteriorate since independence. In Brazil, in São Paulo's industry inflation reduced real earnings by more than 50 per cent at the very moment when there was still talk of the 'Brazilian miracle'.

A second consequence is the formation of a social class capable of consumption thanks to its position in the dependent economy—or even in an expanding local capitalist economy (India, Korea, South Africa, Brazil, Mexico)—or in State or private services. The gulf separating them from the mass of the population steadily increases. In Brazil between 1960 and 1970, for example, the share of national income received by the top 5 per cent of the population rose from 27 per cent to 35 per cent—according to official statistics; unofficial sources say 46 per cent.[20] This is a model found from Thailand to the Philippines, from El Salvador to Chile, from Zaïre to Kenya, wherever a capitalist model of development is followed.

### 3. THE CULTURAL CONSEQUENCES OF DEPENDENCE

Various cultural effects have been mentioned in the preceding pages, but perhaps the most important is the effect of an imposed technology on educational systems. In many countries education was and often still remains a copy of the metropolitan system of the colonial period. The system produces young people, especially in secondary schools, whose main ambition is to leave the country for the towns and not to tie themselves to a manual occupation. The model proposed is to look for a job in the tertiary sector. When a country like Tanzania tries to transform its educational system in order to adapt it to a progressive socialist model of development based on the rural areas, it encounters very strong resistance—particularly from the churches, which are used to having considerable responsibility in this sector. The almost total lack of technical education adapted to the needs of the country is also characteristic of most Latin American countries; the small number of technicians trained is absorbed by foreign companies.

The scholarship policies of western countries also fall clearly into place as part of the policy of increasing economic dependence by slanting education. It is a striking fact that scholarships for social studies have been sharply reduced, and in certain countries even abolished, because they are considered superfluous or even dangerous. The overwhelming majority of those who study abroad return with the passport which allows them to take their place among the privileged minority with every interest in reproducing the established model. Those who identify with the lower classes and fight for their emancipation are few. In the socialist countries education was first democratised and extended to the whole population. It has often been coupled with manual work (in Cuba, Vietnam and Tanzania). On the other hand, while there are many scholarships in the developed socialist countries, efforts to adapt courses to the situations of underdeveloped countries are often inadequate, both in the technological field and in that of the social sciences. This creates inadequacies which may be serious, but are less important in the long term because countries, even underdeveloped ones, have a firmer grasp of the mechanisms of their economic, social and cultural growth.

Cultural dependence also appears in the area of the mass media, the press, radio and television. We need only think of the monopoly enjoyed by the four or five big international press agencies, Agence France Press, Reuter, UPI. However, a more serious factor from the cultural point of view is the domination exercised over radio and television. The case of Zaïre has already been mentioned, but there are many other examples to be added. In Mexico almost all television programmes come from American stations, and this situation is repeated throughout Latin America. In Sri Lanka in just over a year (1979-1980) 60,000 television sets have been sold at prices ranging from $1,600 to $3,200 each when the average income of the population barely reaches $200 a year. Televisions will soon be placed in schools and community centres. 99 per cent of the programmes (apart from local news broadcasts) are imported and advertising is almost exclusively for foreign products.[21] It is not difficult to imagine the values which are transmitted and the potential effect they could have on the attitudes of the population.

When trying to realise the global effect of economic, social and political domination it is useful to refer to an extreme example such as Saigon. Disintegration was so great, particularly in culture and morals, that it will take years, if not a generation, to change things.

CONCLUSIONS

Economics, politics and culture are simply three faces of a single reality. It is impossible to separate these different aspects. Genuine development will only take place when the whole of the population is involved in it and made socially and culturally active. The commercial economy introduces a fundamental fault into the mechanism because it is built on contradictory foundations with these objectives: the accumulation of capital, technical efficiency as a means to profit, the maintenance of domination in markets for raw materials and manufactured goods, of cultural influence and political control. It is also incapable of solving the Third World's development problems. It was estimated in 1972 that to catch up the United States it would take India 200 years, Uganda, Malaysia and Peru 400 and Pakistan 1,750—the commercial economy is actively destructive of the fundamental mechanisms of development. The process can be described in social terms as a gigantic class struggle on a world scale. If we want to say an effective Christian word over this situation, we must first analyse it in realistic terms. As long as the churches do not do this they share objective guilt for the situation, despite the treasures of generosity and good will developed within them. This highlights the dramatic inadequacy of the 'social teaching of the Church', which sees the solution of injustices in a collaboration by all classes in working for the common good without a need to create the conditions for putting an end to the mechanisms of domination we have described.

*Translated by Francis McDonagh*

*Notes*

1.  During the first decade, while the *per capita* income of the developing countries rose by $40, that of the industrial countries rose by $650 (J. Omo-Fadaka), quoted by Amin 'Dependent Development' *Alternatives* II (1976) 381.

2.  *Ibid*. 386.

3.  B. Verhaegen 'Zaïre: les chainons de la dépendance' *Dialogue* (Rwanda) 68 (May-June 1978) 18-20.

4.  *Ibid*. 21-22.

5.  World Bank report, quoted by *Faim-Développement*, Dossier 79-12 (December 1979) 16.

6.  *La Prensa Latina* (Buenos Aires), quoted by ALAI (Agence Latino-américaine d'information, Canada), 27 (29.9.77) 142.

7.  The Confederation was formerly known as the International Confederation of Christian Trade Unions.

8.  Confederation *Flash spécial* 116 (25.10.79).

9.  Suzan George 'Le Tiers-Monde face à ses riches clients' *Le Monde Diplomatique* (March 1979).

10.  Sophie Bessis *L'Arme alimentaire* (Paris 1979) p. 44.

11.  USDA-FAS, quoted by *Faim-Développement*, Dossier 80-3 (March 1980) 11.

12.  *Ibid*. 13.

13.  George McGovern *War Against Want* (New York 1964) p. 25.

14.  *Chile-America* 35-36 (September-October 1977) 42.

15.  G. Fourez 'Transfert de technologie et développement du Tiers-Monde' *La Revue Nouvelle* 70 No. 7-8 (1979) 73-82.

16.  *Faim-Développement*, Dossier 79-12 (December 1979) 18.

17.  Suzan George, quoted in note 9, at 17.

18.  *Faim-Développement*, Dossier 80-3 (March 1980) 10.

19.  *Ibid*. Dossier 79-12 (December 1979) 16.

20.  Ward Morehouse 'Science, technology, autonomy and dependence: a framework for international debate' *Alternatives* IV (1978-79) 389.

21.  Vamida Tarzie Vittachi *Newsweek* (14.7.80).

Kuno Füssel

# The Socio-economic Conditioning of the Church

## 1. THE THEORETICAL FRAMEWORK

1. IF, FOLLOWING the Second Vatican Council, we take the Church's historical nature and involvement in the world seriously,[1] we may use analytical terminology to express that historicity and mundane reference as follows: the structure, characteristics and mode of articulation of the Church are shaped, limited and orientated in accordance with the particular mode of production (MP) that predominates in a specific society. According to Althusser,[2] MP comprises the social production and reproduction process which is defined by at once the relative autonomy and complex unity of its components so that the economic base is ultimately determining; in other words, economic factors decide the point at which the other factors of politics and ideology reach the limit of their specific practices and functions.

Though the Church does not see its purpose (leading people to eternal salvation) as directly social and its forms of action as derived directly from socio-economic circumstances, even if there is a legitimate distinction to be made between the Church's nature and manifestation, nevertheless its necessarily social composition and the class allegiance of its members mean that it is determined by MP antagonisms and the resulting asymmetrical social relations and conflicts between rulers and ruled. Class divisions do not pass the Church by; therefore the ecclesiastical apparatus always consciously or unconsciously assumes certain functions in class conflicts, so that historically the Church has acted both as a guarantor of domination and as a subversive and system-erosive force.

If we accept Engels' view[3] that the superstructure is relatively autonomous and exerts its own influence on the basis, it is not permissible to interpret every ideologico-religious configuration as also being a direct expression of socio-economic conjunctures. In the case of the Church there is always a complicated interaction between specific transformation processes within it and processes of change in other superstructural institutions and the basis of society.

*Hypothesis 1:* Precisely because the Church has assimilated elements (rites, offices, dogmas) from the most varied social formations, it always retains a relative autonomy in relation to other societal factors, and maintains an ambivalent, non-simultaneous relationship to them, with the aim of its own (extended) reproduction having absolute precedence.

11

2. The life of the Church is lived on (*a*) the level of needs and practices, (*b*) that of the institutional apparatus, and (*c*) that of the interpretative system, of values and ideal relations.

*Hypothesis 2:* Accordingly the Church is a structured whole consisting of actors, practices, rules, dogmas and discourses, in which however the ideological level is dominant. Even the drive of the clerical apparatus to possessions, power and knowledge serves these ideological functions and is not, as revolutionary analyses so often assert, an end in itself.

We understand ideology in general as comprising a system of directives on action and explanations which are constitutive of all historical social formations. Ideology does not exist only in the head of the individual but also has a material existence, in so far as the ideas in which the individual believes are 'material actions which become an integral part of material practices controlled by material rituals. These rituals in their turn are determined by the material ideological apparatus on which the ideas of the individual in question depend.'[4] The ideological aspect is dominant in the Church in so far as it makes possible and justifies the functioning in particular of the clerico-political apparatus and its functionaries (bishops and priests) by affording ideal relations of the actors to God/Jesus Christ, and thus primarily constituting these actors as believers and binding them to agreement on all decisive questions.

3. This explains why the ruling classes and the State authority have always shown profound interest in recruiting the Church to confirm or extend their power.

*Hypothesis 3:* Because the Church conceives society as conducted in accordance with general principles and concepts, and therefore tries to inculcate them as behavioural norms in members of society, it is allowed a special ideological competence; its effect is all the more supportive of domination in that it does not openly acknowledge any direct class interest but appears to represent universally valid principles, so that social antitheses tend to be transformed into a struggle between such principles.

It would therefore seem to be advisable for the Church critically to investigate the responsibility for fundamentals which it is accorded by many parties because it is largely redundant. But even if the Church were able successfully to resist the danger of this kind of manipulation, it would still not escape the other danger of indirectly reproducing within itself the asymmetrical structure of social conditions, because it conceives itself as an entity in competition with the existing power bloc, and therefore directs religious production, the circulation of symbolic products (vestments and so on, rites, rubrics and texts) and their consumption in accordance with that bloc's strategies.

Nevertheless the Church does not have a function which is obviously of service or analogous to the existing power bloc; instead, by reason of its origin in Jesus' messianic practice,[5] its effect is properly much more subversive. This, however, presupposes both an epistemological and political severance from the principles of the ruling group. Here lies the function of the theologian as 'an organic intellectual',[6] between the basis and the superstructure, who not only helps the 'culture of silence' of the oppressed to win through, but also gives their position in the class struggle a theoretical expression.

4. The Church's position in the ideological class struggle and the effects of the social content on its attitude may be discerned in the typical instances of official texts, especially the statements of the magisterium.

*Hypothesis 4:* The production of texts is the most influential form of ideological practice. Texts not only influence the conscious mind, because of the ideal reference of their subject-matter, but affect preconscious behaviour because of their nature as a material sign-system. Hence the text itself is a locus of the social nexus and of direct access to societal confrontations. This explains the efficacy of texts and their rôle in the reproduction of the conditions of production by means of the cultural apparatuses which are the family, school, church and media.

2. ANALYSIS OF TWO CHURCH DOCUMENTS

## (a) A document from the Church in the Federal Republic

(i) After the Second World War, through the CDU/CSU (Christian Democratic Union and Christian Social Union) and lay groups and interests obedient to the bishops, and with the aid of a Catholic social doctrine adapted to the economy and an anti-Socialism extended into the realm of metaphysics, German Catholicism succeeded in obtaining political influence and establishing itself as a power in the social order. Therefore the change of government that came about in 1966 meant that the Church's own socio-political position was endangered.

In 1972, when the socially liberal government of the Social Democratic coalition had been in office for three years, the German Bishops' Conference issued a 'Declaration on Social Development in the Federal Republic'.[7]

Basing themselves upon their 'responsibility for the general good', in the preamble to this document the bishops express their concern about the 'increasingly threatening erosion of basic human values', and presume that in saying this that they accord with 'numerous forces of renewal . . . in our people'. In Part I of the document they characterise 'modern society' in terms of the contradiction between personal freedom and State regimentation, accuse the State of a negligent degradation of moral values, and foretell the danger of a 'complaisant democracy' deluded by the dream of 'social Utopias'. But the fact that ultimately it is a question not of a specific notion of the State[8] but of the exercise of State power by the parties in the social liberal coalition, becomes evident if nowhere else at the point where profession of basic moral values becomes undisguised mourning for the end of the Adenauer era: 'In the nineteen-fifties the agreement of decisive legal norms with the moral law was taken as obvious. Today that is no longer the case': in other words, the social liberal coalition promotes moral decadence. Resolutely, therefore, in Part II, devoted to the discussion of 'certain developments', the reader is reminded initially of the discussion of the criminal prosecution of abortion. The bishops try to give the impression that unborn life was more effectively protected by the old paragraph 218 of the legal code than by the revised paragraph, even though hundreds of thousands of abortions in the previous decades demonstrate the exact opposite. A direct line is drawn from the increase in crimes of violence and terrorism to 'political extremism' and 'the proponents of . . . radical ideologies, who have already acquired key-positions in our society and exercise their terror in education, in the mass media, and in politics'. The bishops opine that the 'declared will of the great majority of our nation' (that is, CDU voters, since the CDU is the party of the largest numbers!) entitles them to call here for the retention of authoritative measures. Therefore they are not entirely trustful of the freedom of the individual, and the individual responsibility that otherwise they profess to support is not always what they would recommend. This insistent argumentation for a particular political party is continued on the level of the family, and the 'growing enmity towards the family and children' is criticised without even indicating its deeper causes in the capitalist mode of production. In an appeal to 'those holding responsibility in public life', such persons are in Part III required to 'do everything to ensure that citizens remain free and individually responsible, and are not incapacitated as objects of State care and planning'. In Part IV, the last, where they again address all citizens, the bishops try to emphasise their representation not of special Church interests but of the general good.

(ii) Instead, however, of offering a real social analysis, the bishops combine tendentious indications of current trends with a morality that is not defined with any precision but merely invoked, and put forward this mixture as the supreme standard. An attempt is made to win acceptance of the views asserted not by means of demonstrable evidence but by means of supposed general interests and an underlying fear of chaos. But what could be closer than such a procedure to bourgeois ideology and its application in class war from above?

It is characteristic of the logic of institutionalised ideologies in a bourgeois class society formally to justify one's pronouncements as universally applicable, so that no one can oppose one's claims without a bad conscience.

The assertion of bourgeois class interests in the form of universal norms must necessarily take the shape of a deduction of concrete behavioural rules from supreme and unassailable principles. The legitimacy of the existing conditions of production (that is, ultimately, conditions of ownership of the means of production) is then shown by their appropriateness in regard to certain fundamental ideas and 'sacred basic values'. Catholic social teaching is especially well placed to carry out the overvaluation to the status of principles required by bourgeois ideology. For this purpose it not only holds in readiness such pertinent principles as personality, solidarity, subsidiarity, but can extend the requisite exaggeration even into the realm of the transcendent, so that politically divisive conflicts become literally religious conflicts and Left-wingers intent on changing the system also become atheists and God's enemies.

Nevertheless the West German bishops cannot be accused of supporting State authority as such without any reservation. But they are far from moving in a grass-roots democratic direction, for all they are concerned with is a shake-up of the group in power and thus with an associated assurance of the distribution of property and influence. Their populist appeal to the majority of the people would not be heard if that majority voted for the Socialists and not for the Christian Democrats.

### (b) A document from the Nicaraguan Church

(i) Under the title 'Christian Commitment for a New Nicaragua', the Nicaraguan bishops published a pastoral after the liberation of their country from the grip of the dictator Somoza. This pastoral,[9] dated 17 November 1979, was addressed to priests, religious, basic communities, preachers and all people of good will. The bishops do not begin with instructions, but with what they have learnt from the revolutionary process: 'We have recognised that in the years of suffering and social marginalisation our people acquired the necessary experience for application to inclusive and profoundly liberating action. In heroic struggle our people defended their right to a life of dignity, in peace and justice. This is the real meaning of this action they have lived through against a régime which maimed and suppressed human, personal and social rights. . . . We have recognised that the blood of those who gave their lives in this long struggle, the unstinting effort made by young people for a just society, and the prominent rôle of women (otherwise subject to social discrimination) in this entire process afford new energies for the construction of a new Nicaragua.'

Then, alive to the conflicts associated with economic, political and cultural change and the resulting possibilities of error and abuses, the bishops indicate that the central task of reconstruction demands the active participation of the entire nation.

The bishops' remarks on Socialism[10] place them on the side of the poor as a class. Under German conditions, they would sound 'extremist'.

After rejecting crude descriptions of Socialism, the bishops write: 'If on the other hand Socialism . . . means primacy for the interests of the majority of the Nicaraguan people and the model of a jointly responsible, increasingly participatory and nationally planned economy, then we have no objection. This kind of project of a society which ensures the common application of the products and resources of the country; which makes it possible to improve the quality of human life on this basis of the satisfaction of the fundamental needs of all people, seems just to us. If Socialism implies the progressive removal of injustice and the usual inequalities between town and country, between the wages paid for intellectual and physical labour, if it means the participation of the labourer in the products of his or her labour and the removal of economic alienation, then there is nothing in Christianity to oppose this process.'

In one section the bishops address themselves 'with a word of faith and hope to the present revolutionary process'. They stress the fact that liberation and justice are at the centre of Jesus' proclamation of the kingdom of God. Liberation in Jesus Christ comprises human relations to the natural environment, to one's fellow men and women, and to God. The struggle for love and justice—but especially the unambiguous option for the poor—is concrete thanksgiving for the presence of the liberating power of God in history. A third section speaks of the responsibility of the Nicaraguan Revolution in regard to the fact that so many hopes from all over the world are directed to its successful future.

(ii) In the course of an arduous process of awareness, the Nicaraguan bishops already freed themselves under the rule of Somoza from the embrace of bourgeois ideology and learned to understand that commitment to the poor under certain socio-economic conditions, primarily because of a brutal dictatorship, included an acceptance of revolution, if the liberation of the oppressed was not to remain a pious wish and a 'religion is the opium of the people'. With the acknowledgment of the centrality of the axis oppression/liberation for the self-realisation of the Church too, comes the awakening of a new Christian awareness that the eschatological vocation of the Church to bear practical witness to the inclusive liberation of mankind is to be preferred to a predominantly static and legalistic notion of the Church. The more this new consciousness that the religious promises and the political hope in the liberation of the oppressed classes prevails, the more, however, the poor and marginalised become the preferred location of the presence of Christ. The people no longer remain the object of concerned instruction or paternalist leadership but themselves become the subjects of the realisation of the true Church of Jesus Christ.

### 3.  ECCLESIOLOGICAL CONSEQUENCES

An analysis of texts reveals characteristics which enable the particular ecclesiastical reality to be described as a factor of a social formation.

### (a)  Characteristics of a Church orientated to the superstructure

(i) A Church orientated to the superstructure reproduces the contradictions of the circumambient class society. In the religious and theological production of symbols, texts and so on we have a process analogous to the social division of labour between intellectual and physical labour and to a separation of the people from the religious means of production and to the production of experts and functionaries who alone control the means for the satisfaction of religious needs and their distribution.

The religious producers operate in another social space as religious consumers. This leads to the monopolisation of production on the one hand, and to the pure privatisation of appropriation on the other hand. The results are that religion and theology are no longer the products of a community but remain relegated to specialists and their special interests. The division of labour also means that religious and theological intellectual labour accords more with the way of life of the privileged than with material labour, so that the distance from the ruling groups is automatically less than from the working population. The result is therefore an approximation to the habits and interests of the bloc in power, and the almost obvious assumption of a position of hegemony.

(ii) Accordingly the entire power in the political apparatus of the Church is concentrated on the hierarchy: the pope, bishops and priests. The remainder of the people of God do not share in the central decision processes. The layperson is merely the bearer of secondary ecclesial values. He participates in apostolicity together with the Church only in so far as he submits in faithful obedience to the dispositions of the hierarchy.

(iii) The unity of the Church (as a complex whole composed of contradictions) turns to univocity of doctrine and unification of the symbolic field. Linguistic rules which are distant from reality and intended to introduce uniformity exaggerate social and theological contradictions and are designed to ensure the readiness of the basis to offer a consensus in regard to the hierarchy. Any conflicts which arise are concealed, repressed or attributed to those who reveal them. Before all else the class division of society (and class struggle) is denied. Moral appeals replace concrete commitment and supernatural reconciliation replaces the transformation of the existing conditions of domination.

### (b) Characteristics of a Church orientated to the basis

(i) A Church orientated to the basis[11] is rooted in the underprivileged classes, which are powerless both religiously and politically. In economic terms, too, it therefore becomes a poor Church and cannot be merely a Church for the poor. In opposition to the asymmetrical distribution of products and power in the class society, it is concerned with the construction of a neighbourly society marked by active participation and co-determination. There is a parallel displacement of theology and of theologians towards the people which introduces a structural alteration of the entire theologico-ecclesiastical mode of production. The processes in the basic communities, which organise service of the unity of the Church as horizontal cooperation and not as hierarchical subordination, show how the division of labour between theological producers and religious consumers and the associated conditions of domination resulting from this structural transformation can be overcome, and the social and theoretical conditions of the production of a Church outlook can be re-appropriated by those actually concerned.

(ii) If the people become the bearer of ecclesial reality, that does not mean the abolition of the office of priest or bishop, but only its liberation from superficial sacral bureaucracy. All members of the community are called to serve; every service answers to actual needs; and all are therefore participants in the ecclesiastical power entrusted to the community as a whole. This abolishes the schematic division into a leading élite in whose hands is concentrated the whole decision-making and administrative power, and an army of those who receive and carry out the orders.

(iii) As the Church of Jesus Christ and the apostles is shaped anew in the oppressed class and a Church of the people comes into being, it is also possible to initiate a process of liberation encompassing society as a whole. The Church does not merely cease to participate in the bloc in power, and thus to confirm it, but also helps to abolish social conditions of domination and subordination by means of a mutually responsible form of practice which promotes community, and to establish islands of a classless society within the framework of the existing class society. Thus the basic Church does not only ensure unity with the Church of the Acts of the Apostles and the martyrs, but direction to the universal task of the Church. But there cannot be justice and love for all so long as the poor do not enjoy justice and the oppressed are not liberated.

4. POSTSCRIPT FROM EXPERIENCE

Some days after writing it, the author of this article discovered the accuracy of his assessment of the situation as given in note 8. When taking part in a demonstration of solidarity with El Salvador, in the form of a symbolic search for asylum in Cologne Cathedral, I became a living witness to the unexampled cynicism of German prelates who would rather have a peaceful demonstration brought to an end by police action than utter even a word on the problems of an oppressed people. How poor is the rich Church of the Federal Republic! Saint Romero of El Salvador, pray for us!

*Translated by J. G. Cumming*

*Notes*

1. In the Constitution on the Church, *Lumen gentium*, the Council admits self-critically that the Church's existence in the world affects its own fulfilment: 'In its sacrament and institutions which still belong to this wordly time, the pilgrim Church bears the form of this world which passes away' (§ 48).

2. See L. Althusser *For Marx* (London 1973) esp. pp. 151ff.

3. F. Engels 'Brief an J. Bloch' *Marx-Engels-Werke* (MEW) XXXVII p. 463; G. Girardi 'Christlicher Glaube und Historischer Materialismus' *Korrespondenz der Christen für den Sozialismus* (1980) no. 26 3-22.

4. L. Althusser *Ideologie und ideologische Staatsapparate* (Hamburg and West Berlin 1977) p. 154.

5. See F. Bélo *Lecture matérialiste de l'Evangile de Marc* (Paris 1974) esp. pt. IV.

6. See A. Gramsci *Philosophie der Praxis* (Frankfurt am Main 1967) pp. 405ff.

7. The text is quoted in the version supplied by KNA (23.9.72).

8. The bishops do not give any details of the State activity which they wish to see restricted. In any case, they do not refer to the repressive apparatus of the State (police, military forces, gaols), which they specifically acknowledge in the form of specially appointed clerics.

9. The quotations are taken from the original text: *Carta Pastoral del Episcopado Nicaragüense: Compromiso cristiani para una Nicaragua Nueva.*

10. Unfortunately there has been a growing number of signs recently that a few bishops are becoming less favourable to this openness to Socialism as against the traditional anti-Socialism.

11. On this theme see especially L. Boff *Eclesiogenese. As comunidades eclisais de base reinventam a Igreja* (Rio de Janeiro 1977); *Theologie aus der Praxis des Volkes* ed. F. L. Castillo (Munich & Mainz 1978); N. Greinacher *Die Kirche der Armen* (Munich 1980).

Marie-Dominique Chenu

# A New Birth: Theologians of the Third World

CHRISTIANITY IS an economy, not an ideology. What this means is that it is constituted by 'events' which make up a history, the intelligibility of which can subsequently be formulated in concepts and in a doctrine. The penetration of this intelligibility and this doctrine must remain intimately bound up with the events themselves, the first pole of which that recapitulates all the others is the entry into history of the man-God. Christ 'is the goal of human history, the focal point of the longings of history and of civilisation, the centre of the human race, the joy of every heart, and the answer to all its yearnings' (*Gaudium et Spes* § 45). It follows that all events, great or small, personal and collective, down the centuries and across every region of the world, here take on their supreme meaning for the destiny of men and for the future of the kingdom of God, without detriment to the analysis of their diverse earthly causation.

For some decades now we have been witnesses of and actors in one of the greatest events in the history of humankind, in so far as it is on the way to establishing a new balance of its structures, its cultures, of its cosmic being: the two-thirds of the human race which have for many centuries now been living in dependence on and therefore under the domination of the West are in the process of becoming aware of their personality, of their own values, of their resources and of their human dignity. This Third World, as it is called, is emerging onto the economic, social, political and religious stage of world history. This is an extraordinary mutation, charged with hopes and anguish, an 'event' of much more far-reaching importance than any evolution that has gone before. Now the fact is that Christianity is in the grip of this socio-economic revolution and is engaged in finding a place for it in its economy, not in some accidental way but as part of its substance. This whole issue is devoted to the analysis of this mutation. Our own business here is to take the measure of the dimensions of the mutation in the theology that is secretly at the heart of all the other mutations—to seize what are its living insights, its contexts, its methods, its scope. Shall we not be seeing a new theology—in the way that Latin theology was new in relation to eastern theology—and not merely a prolongation of the theology established in the West?

We can from now on take it for granted that the advancement of the Third World is not going to take place through the First World helping it to catch up nor through a transfer of economic or cultural riches; it requires the development of an indigenous vitality which will enable it to escape from the tutelage of the rich industrial civilisation. The same goes for Christianity: a further extension of an established system will not be enough, what is in question is a 'birth', within the tradition which since the advent of the man-God is the axis of the recapitulation he engaged. What this amounts to saying is that the elements which our analysis discerns are no doubt to be found in the capital of the gospel but that they will take on a vital actualisation which will be in continuity with the classical theologies of the West and nevertheless put them in question. The elements in question are as follows.[1]

## 1. REVEALING HISTORY

The first element, then, in the Christian commotion of the Third World, is the fact that it is occurring in a people which, by a molecular contagion, is taking on its own consistence in its faith and evangelism. Prophets, both lay and clerical, passionate and revered animators, do no doubt emerge, as they always do in times of upheaval in the Christian economy; hierarchical leaders do no doubt frame the instinctive initiatives of communities of faithful into formulations and decisions; but in this particular conjuncture it is the people that feels, in some elemental way, that it is the subject and carrier of the gospel, even where it is the agent of the history of which it becomes aware as it makes it. It is not that it superimposes some religious or dogmatic scheme on the social analysis of economic and political conditions but rather it reads the gospel in the very experience of injustice which oppresses the poor. It does not refer to a God who promulgates commandments for the right order of the world from on high but to a God involved in the concrete history of society and personally provoked by the violence perpetrated on the poor by this society. This entanglement of God in the vicissitudes of men leads us to frame a theology other than that of the Absolute of the deists and, moreover, to dignify these vicissitudes as the place of divinisation. The history of men and the economy of God become correlative. The divinisation of man continues the humanisation of God. Presence to the world, and thereby to the future of the world, become structural features of the Church in its own understanding of itself, since the reality to which the faith adheres is present in the history of the world. The mystery is in history.

If mystery is in history, then history is 'holy'—not, however, by some sacralisation, since it remains profane, nor by some mystical extrapolation which would empty it of its own content, nor by some heterogeneous superstructure, but in virtue of its own terrestrial density and of the autonomy of its causes in the total assumption by Christ. There is only one history: contrary to what those who have been speaking in terms of a differentiation of planes since the Council of Trent were saying, we must retain the dimensions of the same concrete reality, in its eschatological tension. Progress in history does not of itself introduce us to grace any more than it constructs the kingdom of God, for the life which God offers us is given freely in his love and it goes beyond anything we can accomplish in history. That is why we say that the kingdom is of God, that it is grace and that it is his work; but it is not offered to us outside history and cannot do without it (see the Fourth Conference of the Theologians of the Third World, São Paulo, 1980, nos. 35-36). Evangelisation is of a different order from civilisation, but they develop reciprocally. The human enterprise of constructing the world, starting with the feeding of men, the domination of nature, the gathering awareness of the peoples, the installation of justice, the haunting dream of peace, the cultivation of the spirit, are not only occasional matters or an external condition, mere scaffolding; 'participation in the transformation of the world is a constitutitive dimension of the preaching of the gospel' (The Synod of Bishops, 1971).

It follows that the 'events' which are the matter of history enter into the economy of salvation: there is a historical dimension of the faith, there is a theological signification of events, that is to say, facts that go beyond the recurrence of natural phenomena and the banal routine of the institution and introduce something new into the present and even more into the outlook of the future. For over a 1,000 years the constitution and destiny of the Roman Empire had entered into the constitution of the Church. The French Revolution was and has remained an essential co-ordinate of western Christianity even in the latter's long and undiscerning opposition thereto. Nowadays the economic and social advancement of the working classes thanks to their demanding their rights and the entry of women into public life with its accompanying awareness of their dignity, the international banding together of peoples to regulate their conflicts: all these are so many massive events which are staging-posts to the kingdom of God. And the reader will no doubt have recognised in this enumeration the list of the 'signs of the times' which John XXIII presented in his encyclical *Pacem in Terris*.

Now we cannot deny that the rising awareness on the part of the peoples of the Third World and their cries for liberation are among the signs that disclose the challenging presence of the Lord; they represent an 'event' of first importance, the episodes of which we see unfolding year by year. It is truly a sign of the messianic time that two-thirds of mankind should be passing from a state of dependence and dehumanisation to freedom of soul and body. How can such an event fail to put in question a certain architecture of the Church, and, by that same token, theology as the reflective and critical awareness of its commitment? My perception is that those who refuse this theology are just those who paid no attention to the famous Bandung Conference in 1955, which was the first explosion of awareness of and protest against the wretchedness and oppression, the birth certificate of the Third World. These gentlemen were 'absent', enclosed in their super-naturalism which fails to see the singleness of man's vocation and which thereby disjoins liberation from eschatological salvation.

Since the rejection of dualism throws into greater relief the historical incarnation and the effective realisation of revealed truth, the theologian is faced with the problem of his relationship with secular ideologies, temporal options, divergence of tendencies, the techniques of liberating development. One possibility would be to adopt the line of the socio-historic sciences in favour of a secular perspective. Over against this we need to affirm the principle that this one history has to be seen, read and lived from the point of view of the faith, even where this misunderstanding in faith is mediated through a particular interpretation of the politics of liberation. In the light of faith we can discern the saving presence of God and in this way we free both the interpretation of and the option for socio-political realities from all absolutisation. The theologian may not be able to escape from the play of these options or from the impact of ideologies, but he is not imprisoned in them either because he transcends them with that faith of his which cannot be reduced to ideologies. Wherever the Spirit of Christ is, there is liberty. The creation of history by men leaves the Word of God free in its transcendence: a dimension that is essential if history is to be revealing.

## 2. 'PRAXIS' AS A THEOLOGICAL LOCUS

If it is the case that the Word of God finds expression by incarnating itself in history and that it finds its vector in man as a historical creature, it follows that the understanding of this Word—theology—is no longer elaborated primarily on the basis of texts, whether the Scriptures themselves or dogmatic formulations, even though these are juridically regulative, but on the basis of faith actually lived in the Christian community and of the questions provoked by these texts in today's world. We have to go

MARIE-DOMINIQUE CHENU    21

beyond a certain exegetical and historical positivism in order to practise a living integration conditioned by the present situation: we have to make the Word of God speak today. 'Revelation is not communication from above of some knowledge fixed once and for all; it means simultaneously the action of God in history and the believing experience of the People of God which translates itself into an interpretative expression of this action' (Claude Geffré).

The result is a displacement of theological *loci*, that is to say, of theology's living sources and criteria: social practice *praxis*—is a constitutive element in the production of theology in the sense that the textual formulations and the discourse to which they give rise find their full meaning only in the actuality of the faith in the community, and not in the rational elaboration of a faith-object. Nor is this all that novel: the theology of the Fathers of the Church emerged directly out of their pastoral care, and for the masters of the great scholasticism of the middle ages theology was defined as being simultaneously 'speculative' and 'practical'. Now we do not need to speak of the subsidence of the scholastic base for several centuries, involving as it did the reduction of the believer's conduct to an empirical casuistry; we can simply note on the one hand the emergence of new and hitherto unconscious areas of practice and on the other hand the more insistent valuation of the historic dimensions of the faith. We therefore abjure abstract speculation in order to give full scope to the concrete situation of the believer, in terms of both time and space. Pastoral theology that until now was a subordinate segment of theological doctrine now refinds its dignity as a locus of analysis and decision. This is the perspective in which people are elaborating theologies of the world, of science, of development, of liberation, of revolution, all domains occupied by critical reflection conducted in faith. It is clear that such a pastoral theology is charged with intelligence—we could say with 'doctrine' if that were not likely to lead us into abstraction again—the sort of intelligence that emerges out of involvement in the significant struggles of the movement of history and that would like to be part of a community instinct with many practices and concerns of the life of the faith. We cannot fail to note that the Council was conducted, in the spirit of John XXIII, as a pastoral judgment and not as a dogma machine.

Theology on the basis of practice: this does not mean only that it refers to situations in order to discern in them unprecedented questions or to put forward new fields of study; that would be to remain somewhat external. This is the stage at which Vatican II remained when it declared that, thanks to the experiences of past ages, 'the Church herself knows how richly she has profited by the history and development of humanity' (*Gaudium et Spes* § 44). Praxis, if it is genuinely ecclesial practice of the faith, becomes part of the tissue of theology to the point that it enjoys a certain normative authority there. Without detriment to orthodoxy, orthopraxis has its own validity, reflected on in contact with 'the changing situations of this world, under the inspiration of the gospel as a source of renewal' (letter of Paul VI to Cardinal Roy, 1971, no. 42).

What is in question is an inductive rather than a deductive theology, as it has been put very suggestively. We can agree, provided that praxis is not thought of as having an exclusive right to talk about the faith and that deductive theology is not relegated to the status of an ideology, but keeps its capacity to conceptualise by way of the exercise *par excellence* of reason, 'theological reason'. Induction and deduction should operate dialectically in such a way as to allow in the same movement for the lived faith of the community, springing from the foundational event of the gospel, and from the contemporaneity of significant practices. This is no doubt one of the characteristics of the new theology.

Be that as it may be, it is with this method that we can establish honestly that relationship between *knowing* and *doing* which is posed in every discipline but more starkly in Christian existence. The Church has—with some justification, unfortunately—been accused of not practising what it preaches, especially in regard to the building of a better world, to the progress of humanity, to the proclamation of rights, to the liberation of man: its declarations are rhetorical and its appeals moralising, belied as they are by its actions. Nor is it enough to say in response that this insufficiency touches only the economico-social conditions and that it leaves the whole man intact; we have to see that the internal cause of this insufficiency lies in a distorted conception of faith in terms of its being abstract, atemporal, idealist, faith, fallen from on high, authoritarian and without prophetic impact. 'Doing the truth' is the way St John talks about it.

### 3. THE BASIC COMMUNITIES

The community of the Church, in all its human extension, is the subject of this theology. But there is one amongst its many sectors that has a quite special position: the so-called 'basic communities', more of a piece than the others are with the methodological and creative presuppositions which we have described.

They are to be found everywhere, and they are held to be a major event in the present structures of the Church. This is not the place, nor have we the space, to analyse their inspirations, their behaviour, their limitations—or, rather, their conditioning—as well as the benefits of these communities within the great Church. All we want to do here is to underline their specific rôle, in a concrete and historical evangelical theology. They are no doubt groups of believers amongst whom, contrary to the disjunction of the temporal from the spiritual noted above, the process of becoming aware of the problem of the advancement of man and of all men is the occasion of discovering the Word of God; amongst whom the discernment of the 'signs of the times' occurs not in daily life; amongst whom the direct reading of the Bible, innocently of the official formulations of the Church, is the evidence of the presence of the Spirit; amongst whom the active participation of the People of God makes theology come out of its university ivory tower; amongst whom layfolk can act without being commissioned by the clergy; amongst whom, in short, 'the struggles for justice and sharing in the transformation of the world clearly appear to be a constitutive dimension of the preaching of the gospel' (Synod of Bishops, 1971).

The decisive role played by these communities, especially in Brazil (where there are some 80,000) and in several churches in Africa (especially in Zaïre), is a perfect illustration of the genesis' methods, but also the risks of a Third World theology which is bringing new blood into a western theology that until now has enjoyed a monopoly.

### 4. THE POOR: CLIENTS AND WITNESSES OF THE GOOD NEWS

It is entirely by design that we have so far kept implicit the nerve of the theology that the theologians of the Third World are in process of elaborating. It is simply that it is the poor who, according to a law of the gospel, and even of the prophets of the Old Testament, are the true bearers of the great news of liberation, and therefore the qualified witnesses of the messianic message. The Fourth Conference of the Ecumenical Association of the Theologians of the Third World, held at São Paulo in March 1980, described the 'evangelical potential of the poor' (Puebla, n. 1147) in the following way: 'These poor—the oppressed and believing people—announce and manifest the presence of the kingdom of God in the path they take, in the battles they undertake: the new life, the resurrection which becomes manifest in their communities, is the living evidence that God is at work in them. Their love for their brothers and their enemies, their solidarity with each other, disclose the active presence of the love of the Father.

The poor can evangelise because the secrets of the kingdom of God have been revealed to them' (Matt. 11:25-27).

Now poverty—and by that we mean structural as well as personal poverty—is the very condition of the Third World: economic, but also cultural and mental poverty, wherever the domination of the First World has held and still holds it in tutelage. This condition of dominated/dominant is radically condemned by the gospel of brotherhood and equality. Every reaction against it is a step towards the understanding of the divine economy for the construction of the world and for the history of men.

It is, of course, true that salvation is offered to all men, rich as well as poor, powerful as well as weak, learned as well as ignorant, men of every race and culture, and across the political board. Universalism, in love and sharing, is consubstantial with the Christian economy. But the universalism of the proclamation of the gospel is via the historic process and involvement in the liberation of the peoples (the Conference of São Paulo, n. 45). It is inevitable, even normal, that ideologies should have their part to play, at their own level; but the superimposed ideologies do not rob the gospel of its messianism since this gospel, by faith, transcends every historical conjuncture, even where it is involved in mundane conflicts and ideological compromises. The urgency of discernment in no way reduces apostolic radicality and pastoral strategies, not only in evangelisation but in the theology which it implies. Poverty is not the object of a morality of resignation; it is the spring of an evangelical and theologal hope.

The experiences which the people of the Third World are undergoing show even in their derivative applications that the Church will not be the Church unless it is—according to the well-accredited slogan—the Church of the poor. The Church is then reborn amongst a people, the people of God.

*Translated by Iain McGonagle*

*Note*

1. We have decided not to append a bibliography. We should, however, like to refer the reader to articles by G. Gutiérrez and J. Scannone in *Concilium* 93 (1974) and *Concilium* 96 (1974) and to *Concilium* 104 (1977). As for the 'displacement of theology', see the papers of the Colloquium of the Institut Catholique de Paris on this subject, Paris 1977.

c

# PART II

*Historical-Theological Reflections*

Robert Morgan

# The One Fellowship of Churches in the New Testament

THE NEW TESTAMENT answers the Christian Church's need for a story of its origins with a sequel to the fourfold gospel relating the early days in Jerusalem, and a partial account of its mission and expansion. The powerful hold which Acts has exercised upon the Christian imagination from the second century to the present is evidence both of a community's need for a sense of its own identity, and of this plausible narrative's capacity to meet that need. The apostles' witness to Jesus 'in Jerusalem and in all Judea and Samaria and to the end of the earth' (Acts 1:8) is continued above all by Paul as its extension from the holy city proceeds from the gentile centre of Antioch to a natural climax in Rome. Apostolic good-will and good sense overcome threats of friction over food distribution (6:1), circumcision of gentiles (15), and Paul's missionary methods (21:20-26). Troubles come from outside, mainly from the Jews. In the future there will be internal divisions arising from false teaching (20:29f.), but the first generation remains intact, an example and an inspiration to its successors.

## 1. IDEALS AND STRUGGLES

The course of modern historical study of Christian origins over the past 150 years could be charted in terms of the more or less critical stances adopted towards this idealised picture. F. C. Baur's epoch-making essay of 1831 on 'The Church in Corinth, the opposition between Petrine and Pauline Christianity and (the legend of) the Apostle Peter in Rome', challenged, if it did not immediately shatter, the myth of apostolic harmony. The critical demolition of Acts with which Baur began his masterwork on Paul (1845) has remained controversial, but every historian would now give priority to the witness of the authentic Pauline epistles as providing a first-hand account, however fragmentary, of the gentile mission in the '50s.

Used critically and in conjunction with Paul's own record, Acts continues to provide a partial framework for reconstructuring first generation Christianity. But its account of the Jerusalem mother church is notoriously vague; the historian must sift the earlier strata of the gospel tradition and search Paul's letters for indications of what Jewish and gentile Christians believed before and alongside him, how they worshipped and how they were organised. The New Testament as a whole provides evidence of the diversity

27

in Christian life and thought towards the end of the first century, and the theological 'tendency' of Acts provides information about the form of 'third generation Christianity' which was to prove most enduring. Baur's chronology has long since been corrected, and other factors than the Jew-gentile controversy affected the development of early Christian thought; the purpose of Acts was not primarily irenic. But there were conflicts in the first generation, and the particular problem of whether gentile Christians should keep the Mosaic law was a divisive issue which might easily have led to a formal break. That this did not happen perhaps permits us to speak of a 'fellowship of churches in the New Testament'.

### (a) Jews and gentiles

The unity of Jew and gentile in Christ dominated the missionary policy and theology of the only named witness that we overhear at first hand. It is generally assumed that Paul persecuted, and was shortly converted to, a hellenist Christianity that was already critical of the Jewish law. After a long period of 'missing years' (Gal. 1:18-21) we hear of an important meeting in Jerusalem. It assumes very different proportions in Gal. 2 and Acts 15, but both the primary and the secondary sources agree that the gentile mission was recognised. According to Paul the only condition specified was not theological but financial (Gal. 2:1-10). No doubt there was more to this than he makes explicit, but 'the gospel to the uncircumcision' was able to continue without the reversal of policy which the Judaising Christians were demanding. Paul remained a controversial figure, even in prison (Phil. 1:15f.) and after his death. The Pseudo-Clementines testify to the passions he evoked. It is not known whether the collection for the saints by which he set much store and about the reception of which he was clearly worried (Rom. 15:31), was accepted.

One result of this first-generation controversy is that the largely gentile Christian New Testament preserves for the instruction of later generations the ideal of Jews and gentiles united in one church. Ecumenical thought, Jewish-Christian dialogue, and First World-Third World relations can learn from this witness to the ideal, however imperfectly it was ever realised historically. The New Testament does not supply blueprints for the Church to imitate in changed historical situations. It states the ideals and echoes the struggles of early Christian writers who were trying to respond to the gospel through their common life. Provided that this orientation to the gospel itself is respected, their inter-related theory and practice of life in the Church may provoke thought on the appropriate form or forms of Christianity today.

The New Testament contains a wealth of ecclesiological imagery, but very little developed ecclesiological thought. Only Ephesians could be described as an ecclesiological treatise, on the unity of Jewish and gentile Christians in one Church. What Paul warned against in Rom. 11 appears to have happened. The now numerically superior gentile Christians need reminding that in Christ, in the Church, they who were once separated from Christ, alienated from the commonwealth of Israel and strangers to the covenants of promise, have been brought near to God, united with faithful Israel. They are one new man, no longer divided as Jews and gentiles.

Paul himself only adumbrated this theme in the course of considering a different problem, the unbelief of his brethren, his kinsmen by race (Rom. 9:3). But his strenuous missionary efforts to maintain fellowship with the mother church at Jerusalem, 'lest somehow I should be running or had run in vain' (Gal. 2:2) are as eloquent as any theology. His entire activity, 'the daily pressure upon me of my anxiety for all the churches' (2 Cor. 11:28), is living commentary upon the claim that 'there is neither Jew nor Greek, there is neither slave nor free, there is neither male nor female; for you are all one in Christ Jesus' (Gal. 3:28).

Whereas Ephesians, and to some extent Colossians, develop Paul's image of the body of Christ to refer to the universal Church, Romans and 1 Corinthians apply it to the unity in diversity to be found within the local congregation. This reflects the character of these documents, addressed to local churches and (at least in the case of 1 Corinthians) concerned with their specific problems. But the extension of meaning is a natural one. It is supported by Paul's remarks about baptism at 1 Cor. 12:13 and Gal. 3:27, where the unity of Jew and Greek in Christ is heavily underlined. There is one Christian baptism—even though Matt. 28:19 provides evidence of variety in liturgical forms.

There is also only one Christian Eucharist (to borrow the second-century term), though again with a variety of liturgical forms. What Paul says at 1 Cor. 10:17 about the unity of those who share in the one loaf can therefore be appropriately extended beyond the local community. Within a local church, table-fellowship was the point at which the precarious unity between Jewish and gentile Christians was most vulnerable (see Gal. 2:12). As with food offered to idols (1 Cor. 8 and 10) and other disagreements between the weak and the strong (Rom. 14), this was a practical, not merely a theoretical issue. At the practical level it might seem to have little relevance for a more secular culture, but Paul can draw theological principles out of passing issues, and modern readers may extend the application. The behaviour of the rich at the eucharistic assembly (1 Cor. 11:17-22) is a denial of Christian fellowship, and this poses a challenge for Christians in a world-wide Church divided between rich and poor.

The 'certain from James' at Antioch possibly, and Paul's opponents in Galatians and 2 Corinthians certainly, visited these law-free gentile congregations intent on controversy. This disruption of fellowship illuminates two features of both good and bad inter-(local)-church relations: that it depended on travel, and on mutually recognised leaders or figure-heads. The clearest example is Paul himself, but 1 Cor. 9:5 shows that apostolic travel was equally characteristic of the Jewish-Christian mission. Quite apart from the travels of certain leaders, movement of Christians such as Aquila and Priscilla, whether in the course of business or as a result of expulsion, would foster a sense of belonging to a world-wide fellowship. Travel, bearing and sharing (Col. 4:15f.) letters from acknowledged leaders, was the natural and highly personal way in which this developed in the period before local and provincial synods began to provide a wider forum. Intercessions and financial assistance were also both expression and catalyst of this wider fellowship.

The gospels offer nothing directly comparable, on account of their genre, and we are left wondering what contact, if any, the communities in which these were written had with their neighbours in Christ. The Johannine community in particular gives an impression of isolation, but 2 and 3 John show that 'the elder' plans to visit it, and John 21 may contain an oblique warning against the exaggeration of Petrine claims adumbrated in Matthew. It would therefore be rash to assume isolation too easily.

The controversies surrounding Paul's gentile mission provide suggestions for reconstructing the situations in which the gospels were written. Scholarly hypotheses fill any vacuum caused by the lack of available evidence, and Mark, which provides the least solid evidence for redaction criticism, has provoked a variety of hypotheses. The evangelist's criticisms of the disciples may be a hermeneutical device enabling him to combine a post-Easter perspective with a narrative of the ministry (Conzelmann), or they may be a paraenetic device to clarify the nature of Christian discipleship (Schweizer). But they may also reflect a historical situation of Markan hostility to the Jerusalem church (Trocmé, Tyson). Certainly Jerusalem is depicted in negative terms and the family of Jesus receives short shrift in this Galilee-oriented gentile gospel. Another hypothesis, based on the undoubted importance of the passion in Mark, is that the evangelist is attacking opponents who deny its necessity or centrality (Weeden). Paul shows that controversy can be theologically fertile, and there are good reasons for respecting Mark's theological abilities. But we do not even know where he was writing (Rome remains as good a guess as any) and the modern tendency to find conflict everywhere is perhaps partly the product of western European confessional oppositions.


### (b) Post-Temple Churches

If the most natural threat to early Christian fellowship lay on the frontier, theoretically abolished, between Jew and gentile, it is all the more striking how far this burning issue of the first generation had subsided by the third. External factors were partly responsible. The destruction of Jerusalem and relative demise of Jewish Christianity resulted in an essentially gentile Church rather than the ideal unity of Jew and gentile in Christ. None of the four gospels provides certain evidence of authorship, place of origin or date, but Matthew and John provide footholds for the historian seeking to reconstruct the churches out of which and for which they were written. They are the most Jewish and the most anti-Jewish of the gospels, and both the products of highly gifted individuals working in Christian communities closely related to a Judaism that was adjusting to the disaster of C.E. 70. As that Judaism began to define itself more narrowly, both evangelists' Christian groups had probably been recently expelled from the synagogue (in the '80s) and were needing to reassert their own identity in a world which was not after all coming to a rapid end. The most startling fact here is what very different responses were made by two Christian communities at around the same time, and probably at no great distance from one another, perhaps in the neighbourhood of Syrian Antioch.

Geographical proximity does not guarantee cultural or religious identity. Both communities are closely related to Judaism, but probably to different forms of Judaism. Matthew can be aligned with the emerging rabbinic Judaism of Jamnia; John is more readily associated with sectarian and syncretistic strands which contributed to the gnostic maelstrom. Relatedly, these two communities depend on very different early Christian traditions. Matthew's background includes the Q traditions and communities of a Palestinian and Syrian Jesus movement which remembered the teaching and retained strong affinities with the life-style of the historical Jesus. John has preserved some interesting historical data not found in the Synoptics, relating especially to the Baptist, Samaria, and the trial of Jesus, but the religious thrust of this gospel is found elsewhere, in the unhistorical revelatory discourses of Jesus, and behind that in his source's crudely miraculous 'signs'. Such astonishing differences are perhaps intelligible if John and Matthew are the product of very different kinds of local church or sect. A sociological perspective might both help the baffled historian and stimulate theologians to consider how far organisation and even beliefs are shaped by social context.

Matthew looks to Peter as the Church's founding figure (16:16-19) though not as guarantor for its ministry. Occasional hints suggest that Matthew's church was led by 'prophets, wise men and scribes' (23:34, and see 10:41, 13:52; and the warning against 'false prophets' at 7:15, 24:24 implies the existence of genuine ones). 23:8 even contains polemic against the development of a Christian teaching ministry analogous to that of the rabbinate. The parallel to 16:19 at 18:18 suggests that for Matthew whatever doctrinal and disciplinary authority his source attributes to Peter, is given to him as representing the whole community.

The Johannine circle also acknowledged some form of Petrine pastoral primacy (21:15-19), even while appealing to the testimony of another disciple. But the Fourth Gospel shows surprisingly little interest in 'the twelve' (6:67, 70f., 20:24), and only uses the word 'apostle' (in an indefinite sense) at 13:16—in contrast to the Apocalypse

(18:20, 21:14, and see 2:2). The Spirit and authority to forgive is given at 20:23 to all the disciples, including presumably the women.

The Matthean and Johannine churches with their Jewish roots and Jewish Christian past are also similar in being open to gentiles. Matthew can look back to the beginnings of Jesus' ministry in 'Galilee of the gentiles' (4:15) and include in his summation of his book a command to disciple all nations (28:19). His Jewish Christian sources preserve the memory that Jesus' historical ministry was in principle restricted to the lost sheep of the house of Israel (10:5f., 15:24), but the Q tradition also echoes the prophetic hope of the gentiles finally entering the kingdom (8:11). John, too, knows that the historical ministry was mostly limited to Israel, but he depicts some Greeks pressing in (12:20-23), towards the hour of Jesus' glorification when he will be lifted up from the earth and draw all men to himself (v. 32, and see 12:52). The 'other sheep not of this fold' (10:16) are presumably gentiles who by the time the discourse was composed had come to believe as a result of the original disciples' witness (see 17:20).

Like the Johannine, the Matthean community was probably mixed, a new 'nation' to whom the kingdom is given and which is expected to produce its fruits (Matt. 21:43). The same image of the vine or vineyard, with its background allusion to Israel (Isa. 5:1-7; Ps. 80) is found at *Didache* 9 (also probably Syrian and primitive) as well as in John 15, which shares with Matthew a strong ethical concern, but gives it a far more individual application (see v. 8). The Church's continuity with Israel is presupposed in all strands of the New Testament and extends to Matthew's terminology (*ekllesia*, *ethnos*, *eklektoi*). But this does not lead Matthew or John to look much beyond their local situations. It apparently required the stronger personal leadership of an Ignatius in Syria to adopt a larger perspective and speak of a 'catholic Church'.

Whereas the *Didache* is a Church order, and contains concrete instructions, these are far rarer in Matthew and virtually absent from John. One may speak of Matthew's ecclesiological orientation, because with his own local church in view this 'scribe trained for the kingdom' (13:52) tries to show what is involved in 'being a Christian', or disciple. His book aims to fulfil what he sees as his Lord's command to 'teach them to keep all that (Jesus) commanded' through a compilation of the earthly teaching presented in a form which clarifies its abiding significance. But the gospel form allows Matthew little opportunity to say much about the gentile mission adumbrated (or rather, reflected) in his great commission.

The individualism of the Fourth Gospel, relegates ecclesiology to the background. The brethren must serve and love one another as Jesus served and loved them (13:14, 15:12), that they may be one, as the Father is in the Son and the Son in the Father, in mutual indwelling (17:21-25). This is easily given an extended application, and in the ecclesiological thought of the New Testament the universal Church is often in view. But the historical circumstances behind most New Testament writings means that their immediate focus is usually on the local group.

### (c) Gnosticism

The largely unknown communities in which and for which the gospels were written remind the historian how very partial a view of early Christianity is to be obtained from Paul and Acts. But both these and 1 John and perhaps Matthew (7:15-23) provide indications of another kind of division which before the end of the century had become a more serious threat to Christian fellowship than the Judaising controversy. In Acts 20 Luke's Paul warns the Ephesian 'elders' (an anachronism suggesting that Paul had established formalised local ministries, see 14:23) that after his departure there would be internal divisions (20:29f.). In Corinth and perhaps elsewhere the historical Paul faced factions arising from doctrinal as well as ethical problems. These gnosticising tendencies were at first internal to gentile Christianity and have left traces on some of the New Testament documents themselves (Colossians, Ephesians, the Fourth Gospel). But they were soon perceived as incompatible with what was beginning to emerge as orthodoxy, and the New Testament also contains both criticisms and evidence of a breach (Pastorals, 1 John, 2 Peter).

The diversity in both theological formulation and Church organisation (to use a looser word than 'order' for the early period) in the New Testament has undermined the traditional picture of a heresy-free apostolic age preserving 'the faith once delivered to the saints'. Instead of false doctrine subsequently attacking the Church from without, historical study reveals considerable local variation and different developments gradually leading through a process of survival, accommodation and finally expulsion, to the ultimately victorious late second-century consensus of catholic orthodoxy.

Some churches were related through a common apostolic founder or authoritative figure, such as John of Asia (Rev. 1:4). The appeal to acknowledged leaders of the first generation became important on all sides in the subsequent doctrinal struggles. But this proved less effective than the strong local leader representing an important centre and conscious of a wider responsibility, such as Clement of Rome and Ignatius of Antioch.

The monarchical episcopate emerged from the presbyterate in response to the need for strong leadership during a crucial period in the self-destruction of the Church. It did not overcome the theological divisions which made it necessary, but provided the emerging catholic Church with a structure which proved more permanent than the gnostic conventicles and schools which it declared outside its fellowship. It provided for a continuity through episcopal succession which charismatic sects could only achieve if they adopted fixed forms. Some of Paul's spirit-led communities developed institutionally into parts of the catholic Church; others presumably petered out. The more formalised organisation enabled the Church to withstand persecution, reconcile some of its lapsed members (contrast Heb. 6:4) and later contain even monastic enthusiasm within its framework.

## 2. TENSIONS LEADING TO UNITY AND RICHNESS

The dangers which threatened Christian fellowship from within and without were no doubt a source of group solidarity. Nothing unites like a common foe, especially if he is a persecutor. 1 Peter and the Apocalypse illustrate this positive aspect of persecution most clearly. The same is true of the internal theological conflicts. The actual unity of the catholic Church was paradoxically sealed by the disasters which destroyed its ideal unity. The line which Paul refused to draw finally against Judaism was finally drawn, and Jewish Christianity itself became marginal and was finally deemed heretical. Gentile Christianity then presented a more united front—but at great cost to the ideal of a genuinely ecumenical Church embracing Jews and gentiles. Similarly, the exclusion of gnostic Christians, including the avant-garde theologians of the early second century, strengthened the Catholic front—but at a cost. The example of Paul, not to mention Jesus, suggests that the richness, power and attractiveness of the gospel is revealed in and through theological tensions rather than by eliminating these.

For the greater part of the second century the organisational achievement of the catholic Church is more impressive than its theological achievement. In a period of transition marked by numerical weakness, persecution, and theological confusion, it was no mean achievement to survive, to 'guard the deposit' (of tradition), and rule out what was clearly unacceptable. Theological construction could await an Origen. But Christians who look back to the early second century should not confuse emergency measures with the ideal. Retrenchment can only be justified as securing a base for further advance.

Neither second-century orthodoxy nor first-century diversity of doctrine, worship and organisation provide eternally valid ecclesiological models. The structures and continuities preserved by the existence of a New Testament canon and threefold ministry, the main achievements of early and mid-second-century Christianity, have proved their worth as a vehicle for the gospel. On the other hand, historical study has destroyed certain myths about the origins of ecclesiological theory and practice, and freed the Church to discover afresh how the gospel can most effectively be shared today. The contribution of New Testament study has this negative destructive aspect, as well as a positive rôle. Its positive contributions to theological reconstruction will be found in its clarification of the gospel to which these documents bear witness, rather than in the empirical data it can unearth about a past epoch. Ecclesiology stems from an apprehension of the gospel in concrete new situations; it is not read off from past historical models.

The most fundamental, often unstated, presupposition of New Testament ecclesiology is that the Church is one, and that local communities do in fact belong to the larger whole. But this larger whole is defined theologically, not yet institutionally. The ethical admonitions of Paul and John refer directly to the local unity of Christians, and only indirectly to the unity of the whole Church. But the one implies the other and when the Church is thematised, above all in Ephesians, the same dialectic of indicative and imperative is found. The Church is one, whether because it is defined as the people of God or because it is based upon the one foundation, Jesus Christ (1 Cor. 3:11). Christians are brothers and sisters in him, in a fellowship which transcends local boundaries, and are urged to express this in their mutual relations.

The sources and signs of unity in one body and one Spirit are the one Lord, one faith, one baptism, one God and Father of us all (Eph. 4:4-6). It is therefore not diversity in Church order, liturgical or even theological formulation which destroys this, but in the first instance 'turning to a different gospel' which is no gospel (Gal. 1:6f.). What constitute the limits of doctrinal variation is a matter of judgment. Where the New Testament writers provide guidance the criterion is christological. Christian initiation involves the confession that Jesus is Lord, and that confession may be developed in different ways, including recourse to historical data. Docetism is excluded in John 4:2 because denial of Jesus' humanity implies that allegiance is no longer being given to Jesus of Nazareth.

A community which does not find its salvation in Jesus of Nazareth alone (Acts 4:12; John 14:6) can scarcely be called Christian. This implies christological definitions which exclude denials of that gospel. But the New Testament writers are only negatively interested in drawing these limits of Christian fellowship. Their positive witness presupposes a shared tradition which expresses their common Christian faith and life. This included belief in the God of Israel, reflected in their use of the Scriptures; confession of Jesus of Nazareth, crucified under Pontius Pilate (see 1 Tim. 6:13) and vindicated by God in Spirit (Rom. 1:4), the symbolic language of resurrection very soon becoming normative; the practice of baptism and participation in the Lord's Supper; shared prayers, including the Lord's Prayer in its various forms. There soon began a pooling of traditions which led first to the composition of the gospels and then to the formation of a New Testament canon. This latter innovation was a part of the same process which led to a more uniform ministry. Both developments were necessary, and effective; it is hard to imagine the Church without them, though the canon allows considerable flexibility in its interpretation and the threefold ministry in its organisation. But the canon is secondary to the material it preserves and the ministry to the ends it serves. Recognition of their historical contingency does not exclude belief in their God-given necessity, but invites freedom, responsibility and willingness to be led by the Spirit in using them in new ways to 'disciple all nations' today.

Agnes Cunningham

# Developing Church-forms in the Post-Apostolic Period

A LIVELY interest in 'models' or 'forms' of Church has developed throughout Christianity in recent years. Reasons for this interest are multiple and varied: new hermeneutical methods, the emergence of historical theology, the reaffirmation of biblical images and designations in the Second Vatican Council's understanding of the mystery of the Church of Christ, ecumenical dialogues, the experience of women, heightened ecclesial consciousness in Christian communities of the non-western world, concern for justice and human rights.

We are increasingly aware that the unity of the Church is not immune to the manipulation and domination of nations divided against themselves in international relationships. We perceive that the diversity which testifies to the redemption of all peoples is too easily threatened by the human nostalgia for uniformity and identity in a Church which is 'the same throughout the world'. We are suspicious of local or 'national' churches whose claims for needs and rights would seem to diminish the universal (καθολικός) character of the whole community of faith.

Why return to the post-apostolic period for light, at a moment when contemporary issues and concerns plague and challenge us? Why expect to find in the writings of the Fathers of the Church answers to questions that derive from contemporary experiences? These questions verge on the rhetorical. A growing body of literature bears witness to the fact that exploration of the past ought to lead to a shaping of the future. In addressing ourselves to the writers of the post-apostolic age and in consulting texts from that period, we can discover the possibility of interpenetrating the structures of the Church at a time when their very fluidity permits the disclosure of what might be called the 'genetic' incarnation of the realities of Christian faith.[1]

In the following pages, I propose to present three basic Church-forms which developed in the post-apostolic period; to examine their presumed fidelity to an understanding of the gospel-message and an experience of the Christ-Event; to suggest meanings and implications they hold for the life of the Church today.

## 1. THE HERITAGE

The Christians of the early post-apostolic age inherited a threefold perception of Church from the oral and written materials that would eventually constitute the New

34

Testament *corpus*. The Church is *People of God, Body of Christ, Temple of the Holy Spirit*. These designations were to contribute significant, constituent elements to the ecclesiological concepts of the Church Fathers. However, they were not exclusively constitutive of such concepts. The Church-forms of the post-apostolic or patristic period manifest the influence of both the creative presence of the Spirit of God and the political-cultural context of specific times and places. These influences provided for the *unity* and the *diversity* of early developing Church-forms. They were the occasion of tension, as Christians struggled to understand the *universality* of the Church in the light of separate orders and experiences in the particular churches.

## 2. THE FORMS OF UNITY

### (a) Doctrine

From the beginning of the post-apostolic period, *unity* is affirmed as an essential form of the Church. In unity, the Church 'assembled with one accord' cries out 'as with one voice' to the Lord (Clement of Rome). Those who break the 'same Bread' are to share an 'undivided mind', united 'in flesh and in spirit' through the observance of the Lord's commandments, living as one 'in a single body, that is, His Church' (Ignatius of Antioch). This unity transcends time and space, generations and nations, embracing all the just since Adam (Augustine, Irenaeus), along with believers scattered through the nations of the entire world (Irenaeus), one in the one Church as Christ has intended it to be (Cyprian of Carthage). The members of this Church are to be one in unity of faith and love, mind and understanding.

The patristic affirmation of unity as an essential Church-form deepened the foundation of the doctrine of the Mystical Body of Christ. In the Fathers, this teaching is uneven and largely implicit. With the Greeks, emphasis is repeatedly on the unity of an inner life which proceeds from God and is guaranteed by incorporation in Christ for visible expression in ecclesiastical unity. Ecclesiastical unity lies at the heart of the mystery of the Church. In the West, especially with Augustine, the Latin Fathers taught a theology of the Mystical Body in terms of the question of grace. The Fathers of the West sought to explain the consequences in human life and action of the unity shared by all in Christ.[2]

### (b) Expressions

The essential unity of the Church found expression in the post-apostolic age in forms that touched the structures of the Church: faith, worship, social organisation.[3] Central to this expression was the Eucharist, 'the medicine of immortality, the antidote against death, and everlasting life in Jesus Christ' (Ignatius of Antioch). Nourished by the Eucharist, the Church in its many members 'is refreshed and grows, is compacted and welded together' (Clement of Alexandria). It was in view of Eucharist that catechumens were instructed and baptised (Justin Martyr), that the Canon of Truth (Irenaeus) and the Rule of Faith (Tertullian) were confided to the members of the believing assembly. It was in Christian worship that the 'body united by a common religious profession' was impelled to a life of almsgiving, discipline and love (Tertullian).

In addition to the one baptism, the one Eucharist and the shared profession of faith, the unity of the Church was reflected in Church order and governance. As early as Clement of Rome, we find a delineation of hierarchical offices and functions (I Cor. 40). The development of the catechumenate confirmed the external standards for determining what it meant to be a Christian. The apostolic succession was understood to have established legitimate authority in the Church and to assure its transmission through the 'tradition of the apostles made manifest in the whole world' (Irenaeus). The unity of each particular Church is preserved through communion with the local bishop, for the 'episcopate is one, each part of which is held by each one for the whole' (Cyprian of Carthage).

### (c) Reflection

In the post-apostolic age, unity, as an essential element of the Church, assumed those Church-forms which were perceived as expressions of the reality of the Christian assembly (*ekklesia*). It was necessary that these forms of unity be faithful to the teaching received from Jesus Christ through the apostles and their successors and that they permit Christians to live as members of an established society in which they had responsible roles to play.

The efforts to achieve this twofold fidelity are reflected in the many images and symbols chosen by early Christian writers to speak of ecclesiastical unity. Each of these symbols reveals the transcendent dimension of a spiritual reality which is the foundation of all unity in the Church: the unity of God in Trinity; the unity of the Person of Christ. Each of the symbols also reflects an attitude or mentality formed in a given culture, accustomed to a specific vocabulary, world-view or recognisable categories of thought.

The unity of the Church is like that of a healthy human body, a well-disciplined army, the ordered movement of planets and stars (Clement of Rome). It is like a great symphony of praise from a choir singing to the Father (Ignatius of Antioch). It is a mighty tower whose structure seems 'to be of one single stone' (Hermas). It is like the sun, 'God's creature . . . one and the same in all the world' (Irenaeus). The forms of unity resemble one flock of sheep, one tree with many boughs, one stream flowing in abundance from a unique source (Cyprian of Carthage). The unity of the Church cannot be broken any more than the 'divine stability' from which it derives. It is entrusted to Christians who live 'in the world' as 'the soul is in the body', assuring life and mobility, proclaiming future life and incorruptibility (*Diognetus*).

### 3. THE FORMS OF DIVERSITY

### (a) Doctrine

The Church-forms of unity in the post-apostolic period contained within their structures the seeds of a necessary *diversity*. The Eucharist itself is the first witness to this reality. From the text of the *Didache* to the Liturgies of John Chrysostom and Basil the Great, we find a transformation that is both enriching and complex in the diversity of theological intuition and understanding, as well as in ritual and practice, even though essentials remain unchanged.

The patristic teaching on diversity as a viable Church-form is limited, as we might expect, in an age when such emphasis as we have seen was placed on unity, in the face of threatening schisms and heresies. There are, however, several key moments of such teaching. About the year A.D. 155, Polycarp of Smyrna appealed to St John and the apostles for the quartodeciman celebration of Easter, against the authority of Anicetus, Bishop of Rome. Over twenty years later, Irenaeus of Lyons, on the authority of apostolic succession, defended the right of particular churches to follow a diversified discipline, exemplified in the Easter controversy. The principle at stake was that unity of faith does not require uniformity of *praxis*. The principle was upheld.

A less felicitous doctrine was promulgated by Cyprian of Carthage in his defence of the autonomy of the local bishop, even in opposition to the Bishop of Rome. Struggles with heretics and schismatics who claimed to be Christian, members of the Church of Christ, encouraged the Fathers in their efforts to affirm a healthy diversity, while preserving the fundamental, essential unity of the Church.

### (b) Expressions

As we have seen, the Eucharist was the primary model of a diversified celebration of worship, within the parameters understood as essential to assure fidelity to the Lord's command. The catechumenate, also, differed in its structures and rites from church to church, as Egeria's *Diary*, among other documents, testifies. The great diversity that prevailed among baptismal Creeds is a well-known chapter in the history of the evolution of the Symbol of the faith.

Further expressions of diversity were found in the constitution of the hierarchy and the ministry of the churches. That hierarchy existed in the churches cannot be disputed. However, members of the hierarchy differed from place to place and from one time to another, in some instances, following the evolution of the presbyterate as a separate order from the episcopate. The development and disappearance of other ministers affected both membership in the hierarchy and services offered in the local communities. For example, there is evidence that women were counted among the clergy in some churches, either as members of the Order of Widows or as deacons. Directors of the catechetical schools (*didascalia*) and prophets were acknowledged, also, as ministers along with others who served the gospel in one manner or another.

### (c) Reflection

The diversity of the Church in the post-apostolic period seems to emerge more clearly as the early Fathers sought to clarify and expand their teachings on the unity of the Church. Paradoxically, the forms of diversity developed within the very forms that called the Church to unity, both internal and external: the affirmation and profession of faith, celebration of Eucharist and 'sacramental' life, members and functions of hierarchy. The ability to sustain and integrate diversity allowed the Christian communities of the patristic era to move towards an understanding of the nature and mission of the *ekklesia*. All peoples, all human history, all human experience would be recapitulated in Christ and brought to the Father, as time unfolded towards eternity (Irenaeus). Nothing of interest to the human intelligence was to be foreign to those who knew the gospel (Clement of Alexandria, Origen). Christians are residents of two worlds (*Diognetus*), inhabitants of two cities (Augustine) which compenetrate each other. It is our responsibility to further the coming of the Reign of God through the means he has placed at our disposal: evangelisation and catechesis.

#### 4. THE FORMS OF UNIVERSALITY

### (a) Doctrine

Catholicity is distinct from unity, in that it refers to the world-wide extension of the Church and the presence of the gospel in every place and in all ages. Catholicity affirms and is rooted in unity. It also assures diversity, incorporating the specifics that transcend any one time or space into the continuity of the Good News, as it is ever proclaimed and lived.

The first use of the word 'catholic' occurs in the writings of Ignatius of Antioch. While he seems to apply the term 'catholic Church' to particular churches, he insists on the unity of these in the one Church which exists throughout the world. The Fathers understood that the Church is 'catholic', that is, universal, as opposed to the localisation of heretical or schismatic sects (Clement of Alexandria). This universality is, essentially, visible (Cyril of Jerusalem, Augustine). The universality of the Church is guaranteed by the unity of faith and government (Augustine). In fact, universality is one mode of expressing unity.

### (b) Expressions

The universality of the Church, as the Fathers taught, is guaranteed by the unity of faith and government. Thus, faith and government, or authority, constitute two forms of expressing the catholicity/universality of the Church. The universality of faith is manifested in the development of doctrine in local and regional Synods and, especially, in the Great Councils: Nicaea I, Constantinople I, Ephesus, Chalcedon. As the faith of the *ekklesia* sought clarification in formulation and theological explicitation, Christological and trinitarian doctrines became the Church-forms which assured both unity and catholicity in the entire Christian community.

Another expression of the universality of the Church surfaces in the role of the Bishop of Rome, both in his own right and in his relationship with other bishops. Following Clement of Rome, the leadership of bishops in other centres of Christianity seems to have overshadowed the successors of St Peter, at least until Leo I and Gregory the Great. Nevertheless, testimony to the uniqueness of the Church of Rome is far from neglected (Ignatius of Antioch, Irenaeus, Cyprian of Carthage, Augustine, Nicaea I, Ephesus, Chalcedon).

The sacramental life of the Church, especially in baptism and Eucharist, was another expression of universality in ecclesial growth, vitality and worship. The witness of the martyrs and of eremetical or monastic commitment and holiness were striking forms of universality where the Church was to be found.

### (c) Reflections

While the original meaning of the word 'catholic' was 'universal' in a 'general' sense, it was used in the post-apostolic age to emphasise the universal character of the Church, as opposed to the particularity of individual congregations and, above all, to the localised character of heretical/schismatic sects.

Catholicity, or universality, as a Church-form was understood to be rooted in the mandate of the Lord as he sent the apostles out to proclaim the Good News to all peoples. The fidelity of Christians to this mandate was restricted, in the pre-Constantinian era, by the antagonism and persecution directed against the Church. With the recognition of Christianity as the religion of the Empire, the followers of Jesus were able to integrate their mission into the structures of the political order in a new way. They also found in an accepting society the models for fostering and modifying Church-forms hitherto developed for purposes of sur/ival and witness through martyrdom.

The debate over the advantages or disadvantages of the 'Romanisation' of Christianity is not germane to the purposes of this article. That moment has been recalled here simply to provide an insight into the development of Church-forms that were 'catholic' in ways that were to influence the subsequent life and history of the Church. In fact, it is because of the development of the concept of universality in the

West, in terms of unity rather than of diversity, that we have attempted to examine those ecclesial forms of another age, in search of a greater understanding of the form of the Church that is perceived so often today as monolithic and uniform in its structures.

## 5. IMPLICATIONS

In the first three centuries of the Christian era, a number of churches emerged as significant centres of Christian life and thought. From these churches came leaders who were outstanding theologians and pastors, liturgical innovation and adaptation, new models of holiness. Jerusalem, Antioch in Syria, Ephesus, Alexandria, Rome, Carthage in Africa, Lyons in Gaul were the great churches of the post-apostolic period. In each of them we find a unique, distinct Church-form, one that could never be confused with any other. However, the underlying foundations and the formative structures of these churches were the same: unity, diversity, universality. Thus, each was unique and each was Christian.

In every age the gospel must be proclaimed in such a way that new church communities are called into being and existing church communities are summoned to renewal. In this twofold process, the formation or reformation of Church-forms is of primary importance. The Church of Christ is to be one in faithful unity, in multiple and enriching diversity, in mandated and missioning universality. Christians must be faithful to the heritage of Word and Sacrament and Tradition which is meant to be alive in every age, even as it is rooted in its origins. Christians must also be faithful to the experiences of humanity in the age and culture to which they belong. The Church-forms of unity, diversity and universality which developed in the post-apostolic age into centres such as Jerusalem and Antioch, Ephesus and Alexandria, Rome, Carthage and Lyons are our assurance and promise from the past for the shaping of the Church for the future. It remains for us to be faithful.

## Notes

1. See C. Kannengiesser 'Avenir des traditions fondatrices' *Recherches de Science Religiene* 65 No. 1 (January-March 1977) 140-141, 142 n. 2, 143.

2. See J. N. D. Kelly *Early Christian Doctrines* (New York 1960) pp. 189-219, 401-421; Emile Mersch S.J. *The Whole Christ* (New York 1938) pp. 209-441.

3. See Y. Congar O.P. 'Structures essentielles pour l'Eglise de demain' in the French language edition of *Concilium* 60 (Supplement, December 1970).

Dorothy Folliard

# The Carolingian Reform:
# Uniformity for the Sake of Unity

## 1. THE CENTRALISING MOMENT

THE LORD told us that his Father's house has many mansions. But his followers have often felt that all should live in only one. The writings of the Apostolic Age reveal divergences of practice and belief. On the necessity of orthodoxy there was agreement—not, however, on content and expression of faith. When the official Church entered the middle ages, it possessed not only a coherent body of teachings, but also an organisation to propagate them and a coercive discipline to maintain them. The spectre of a Roman Empire—'one world' means 'one way'—has haunted the Church. Cultural seedlings of centuries in the many institutional forms and traditions have developed into a jungle growth that has often choked off evangelising efforts which sought to incorporate the innovative and the indigenous. If Caesar had created an empire of *this world*, could not the Church be considered an empire *of Christ* in which the world would be contained?[1]

This study is a glance at that centralising moment, the period of the Carolingian Reform, which we of the West have often called 'the birth' of Europe. Our sources are limited; our world-view is far distant from that of these early medieval Christians. In our childhood naïvete, we have listened avidly to stories of the spread of the faith, the trials and martyrdom of the missionaries who carried it from one barbarian court to another, persuading kings who persuaded their people of the superiority of the Christian God and the credibility of his cult. We regret now that chronicles such as that of Bede do not include descriptions of the gospel values already present in these 'barbarian religions'. This period, often seen pejoratively as merely derivative, was actually creative and life-giving for that time, but the models became absolutised and were destructive in later ages.

In the late eighth and early ninth centuries, uniformity for the sake of unity was profoundly beneficial: 'The uniqueness of the Christian West will never be sufficiently extolled. For all the various races which came into contact with it during the long migration of peoples, it incarnated both the spirit of ancient Greece and Rome and the spirit of the Christian faith.'[2] What was to become 'the Christian West' was then the scene of different migrating tribes now settling. Diversity of pagan cultures, tongues and religions was hindering religious, social and political life. Illiteracy and illegibility of many scripts prevented communication and the sharing of knowledge. The multiplicity

40

of natural divisions impeded communication and the sharing of knowledge. Byzantium, Islam and hostile European tribes threatened the authority of the pope and the unity of Christianity. The situation was ripe for a Charlemagne motivated both by a quest for power and a desire for a deeper Christianity.

The questions had to be: How do many tribes become one people? What is minimal for Christian unity? At this moment, tribal loyalty and rootedness could have meant that baptism had changed little or nothing. The Reform called tribes into sharing symbols common to more than their own group, into a faith that could transcend tribal limitations. Uniformity was crucial at that moment. The clans could never come together unless there were commonalities; a concrete project was necessary if Christianity was to have real meaning.

As faith became incarnated in Germanic Europe, the process of initiation into faith changed drastically. In early Christianity, one became Christian after being personally convinced of the truth of Christianity. But in the conversion of the Germanic tribes, membership in a clan, loyalty to a leader, material advantages, political pressure and physical force became factors in conversion. No sharp break with the past or with the surrounding society was entailed. The Church assimilated thousands quickly, with little interaction between baptiser and baptised.

## 2. THE PROCESS OF UNIFICATION

Out of many themes important in describing the creation of 'uniformity for the sake of unity', three are to be treated here as significant: the reshaping of Roman institutions for a Franco-Germanic society; the adoption of the Roman Rite in liturgy; and, finally, the indigenised evangelisation of these Carolingian Christians. Each aspect is characterised by a borrowing from the Christian Roman world which is claimed creatively and incarnated culturally in a new context. The genetic qualities of early Christianity were not entirely absent.[3]

### (a) Unity through Uniform Institutions

Roman institutions used to unify the Empire in classical times were transplanted and reshaped. The idea of a unified *religious* life was amalgamated to that of a unified political and social life. The personal force of Charlemagne, the Rex-Sacerdos with his plan of political Augustinianism, alone could make it successful. He centralised each sector of society, tying the authority of the archbishop to that of Rome, developing the leadership of the indigenous clergy, calling for obedience from a populace that was sometimes only nominally Christian. But the bond with Rome was magisterial, rather than jurisdictional and legislative. There was much that was innovative—and successful—in the light of the aims of the Reform. Every diocese was given a bishop. Penitential discipline was inaugurated, incorporating Germanic practices. The king's rôle was seen as a fusion of Germanic protecting authority with Roman *tutela*. Frankish councils, the main organ of social programmes, made the bishop the protector of the poor. All of Frankish society was to be regenerated on exclusively Christian lines, with Roman antecedents and Carolingian innovations, forming a new entity: this was no mere restoration.

In the area of law, however, the orientation towards Rome was not without its drawbacks. Most of the laws incorporated in the various Germanic folk laws had rested on the consent of the people, or, at least, of the nobility. As the king became the source of law, the folk laws were not changed, but they were replaced by *capitularia per se scribenda*, the will of the king alone. Laws increased in size and scope; in this ecclesially inspired society, *they became doctrinal statements.*[4]

The antecedents of uniformity without underlying unity are here: the Carolingian model for the West prevailed long after it ceased to be useful and congruent. But to some, the creation has a brighter side: 'The effects were to be felt beyond the original boundaries. . . . This reform is not simply the imposition of a "national Church", an "irruption of Germanism into Canon Law". . . . The achievement of the Carolingian canonists was that they again enhanced the prestige of the canonical tradition of the ancient Church; moulding that tradition to *their* ideas. But without them, the Latin Church might have disintegrated without them into individual churches; at least, the ties of unity might have been dangerously loosened.'[5]

### (b) Unity through Uniform Liturgy

Papal ideas infiltrated rapidly into Charlemagne's realm, not only in ecclesiastical discipline, but also into the life of worship. Out of a rich, but confusing, diversity of liturgies, folklore and languages came a liturgical 'fresh start', centred on the universal adoption of the authentic Roman Rite. The Roman simplicity, sobriety and brevity contrasted sharply with the exuberant, affective devotional style of the Franks. Forty per cent of the liturgical texts adopted are genuinely Roman; the rest is Gallican or semi-Gallicanised.[6] This was a decisive point in the western liturgical synthesis.

The development of a fairly homogeneous liturgy on the Roman pattern was limited, for soon the prayers and the Votive Masses became coloured by the needs of the Carolingian community, which had created for itself a religious mode of life all its own. Indigenisation did not mean slavish imitation.

There was a valuable by-product. As the liturgy assumed its nearly definitive form, the Franco-German Church succeeded in saving the Roman liturgy, an event of invaluable historical importance. For, clearly seen in the hybridisation are shifts towards a liturgy of personal, rather than communal piety—this would represent an intrinsic change in eucharistic worship as it had been understood.

The 'Western Rite', which developed at the time of the Carolingian Reform, thus required conformity, but also encouraged originality. Whereas some uniformity is essential for universality, absolute uniformity denies the very universality of Christianity which liturgy seeks to celebrate. The Carolingian Reform sought concrete expressions of the minimum which could universalise the particular. Highly centralised religious orders later promoted absolute conformity. Adaptive change gave way to obsolescence as the 'freezing effect' took hold and later indigenisations were forbidden.

### (c) Unity through Uniform Evangelisation

In the sphere of Charlemagne, accepting Christ did not mean totally abandoning the German Pantheon. Almost any practice sanctioned by local usage was embodied in Christian life. Popular concepts were tolerated by the official Church and, while old superstitions persisted, evangelisation proceeded, directed towards bringing the people into a full Christian life. Latin and the vernacular were juxtaposed. Sermons, ideally based on the Scriptures and the writings of the Fathers, were delivered in the native tongue. Biblical materials were 'Germanised'. In the poem, the *Heliand*, Christ and his disciples are depicted as a German *comitatus*. Among the oldest texts in German are the 'Our Father', the Creed, the Doxology, lists of sins and formulas for Confession. The 'seeds of the gospel' were seen in locally-based cults and veneration of the saints was understood as enhancing Christ, the heavenly King. The Church continued to purify the expressions of faith from all pagan practices which could not be seen as valid practices of authentic Christianity. Evangelisation continued, emphasising the moral, rather than the intellectual, content of the faith.

Under the great educator, the Church, the Franco-Germanic peoples arrived ultimately at a deeply-rooted faith, a consciousness of sin, a readiness to do penance, a remarkable spirit of sacrifice and charity. The Church never became for them solely an institution—it was the Body of Christ in which he lived and still worked. Combined with the urgency of social responsibility in their own time, this evangelisation was deeply penetrated by the eschatological, as was that of the early Christians.

The uniform evangelisation process, based on a healthy traditionalism and a veneration for gospel values inherent in the culture, was progressive. But subsequent catechesis did not always show progressive development. Tutelage, western institutions, the 'saving of souls'—concepts at home in the Carolingian world-view—were ossified and handed down in a heavy-handed way that devalued the 'seeds of the gospel' in other cultures.

### 3. CONSEQUENCES

Ambitious and premature, and ultimately a failure, this attempt to restore the Roman Empire as the foundation of the new Europe has a religious and symbolic value which far outweighs its immediate importance. For it inspired the dream of a fused religion and empire, of a unified secular and spiritual power. Once developed, the dream persisted and the subsequent demands for unity through absolute uniformity became a perversion of the goals of the Carolingians. The ideal was misinterpreted. Later evangelisations did not provide for the interplay of gospel and culture, did not even envision the indigenous expression of Christianity or the indestructible character that develops slowly from the native force of a people. The ghost of absolute conformity as the only sign and source of unity will not only continue to plague the Church, but will prevent the essential unity of the spirit of diversely incarnated faith.

The creative enterprise of one moment of history, when absolutised, de-historicised, and idealised becomes an obstacle, even a curse, to the ongoing incarnation of Christianity as it moves into new lands and encounters new people. Buhlmann, having assessed as valuable for its time the contribution of the 'Second Church', embryonic in the Carolingian Reform, continues: 'It therefore seems to me that the future can best be thought of in terms of the West being relieved of its present responsibilities. In fact, our present-day experience is that the world's centre of gravity is no longer in Europe. . . . In carrying through with courage the transition from western Church to world-wide Church—all this is the death and resurrection of the Christian West.'[7]

### Notes

1. The uniformity, understandably, was for the sake of *discipline* during the Carolingian period and for the following three centuries. Centralisation of authority prevented lay investiture—the case of Henry IV and Hildebrand comes to mind—and provided for the choice of good bishops. Liturgical life was influenced beneficially. Decretals from the pope, in which individual decisions evolved towards a body of law, had a profound effect. Real inculturation in mission lands was prohibited by the prolongation of these forms.
2. W. Buhlmann *The Coming of the Third Church* (Maryknoll 1977) p. 18.
3. The term is that of C. Kannengiesser in 'Avenir des traditions fondatrices' *Rech. de Sc. Rel.* 65 No. 1 (January-March 1977).
4. See W. Ullmann *Law and Politics in the Middle Ages* (Ithaca 1975) p. 204.
5. H. Fuhrmann 'The History of Canon Law' *New Catholic Encyclopaedia* III 27-28.
6. See G. Dix *The Shape of the Liturgy* (Westminster 1945) pp. 579-580.
7. pp. 18-19.

Enrique Dussel

# The Expansion of Christendom, its Crisis and the Present Moment

THE EXPANSION of Christianity from the fourteenth century onwards, that is to say in modern times, had many positive aspects, but also a fundamental limitation. It was the expansion of Christendom, as a total historical package, which included, implicitly although not always explicitly, the Christian religion, the churches (first the Catholic, then the Protestant from the eighteenth century onwards). Kierkegaard criticised Christendom in the name of Christianity. Christendom was the 'making worldly' of Christianity, making it a Church identified with the State, a 'positive', objectified, alienated Christianity.[1] The prophet of Copenhagen based his criticism on the subjective, internal values of tormented individuality which called for a 'world turned upside down'.[2] In fact Christianity is Christendom turned upside down, but perhaps this inversion should have a more radical, essential basis.

### 1. PRIMITIVE POPULAR CHRISTIANITY AND THE BIRTH OF CHRISTENDOM[3]

As we have seen from previous contributions, the Christian communities scattered throughout the Roman Empire performed their task of evangelising in an exemplary manner. Among the oppressed classes in the Empire (slaves, slum dwellers in the cities, exiles, etc.), they preached the gospel even when they had to brave the hostility of the State. In fact the persecutions were a sign that the Church threatened the ideological hegemony of the Roman State, by denying the consensus of civil society which accepted the State's authority. During its first three centuries, the Church gained acceptance among the oppressed and did not compromise in any way with the repressive apparatus of the State which maintained a system of slavery. In its pastoral practice the Church had a 'model', a 'model' of a 'people's Church'.

But from the moment that the Church attained first liberty and then dominance within the Empire, in the fourth century, a different 'model' of it appeared. *It was not a different Church* but it conceived itself differently in its relations with the world. The 'model' of *Christendom* (which now emerged as distinct from the 'people's Church') situated its hierarchical structures within the political establishment. The State began to control the Church (like the Emperor of Constantinople, Charlemagne, the *Reyes Catolicos* (Ferdinand and Isabella of Spain) or the King of England in the case of the

44

Church of England, etc.). And at the same time the Church received support (military, economic, etc.) for its pastoral practice among the 'Christian people' (who were now thought of as a more or less passive mass of 'laity'). The Church guaranteed the consensus of civil society in its acceptance of the authority of the State; the State guaranteed the Church's exclusive dominance in religious matters within its frontiers. The ecclesiastical structure tended to link itself to the ruling class in the particular society and thus gave its support and blessing to the ruling social order which was sometimes oppressive. Thus it blessed feudalism and later on colonial capitalism. The ruled and dominated, although they were the 'Christian people', had to suffer 'he contradiction of submitting to this domination, which they were told was based \n Christian principles. This 'model' of Christendom is a long way from the gospel an l from Christianity. Christianity has been caught in a structure which enslaves and uses it. This is the subject of this article: the equivocal situation of Christianity since the fourteenth century, when European Christendom expanded throughout the world (Latin America, Africa and Asia), preaching the gospel at the same time as it strove for the expansion of capital: gold and silver for the Iberians, slaves and primary materials for the English, Dutch and French, and every type of merchandise that made possible the increase in industrial or financial capital from the end of the nineteenth century.[4]

## 2. MERCANTILE CONQUISTADOR EXPANSION OF IBERIAN CHRISTENDOM

In Spain and Portugal, as in no other European kingdoms, there were the geopolitical, military, economic and religious conditions for the *reconquest* of their own territories from the Arabs (which was completed by the taking of Granada in 1492), to be continued in the conquest of the rest of the world. Spanish and Portuguese Christendom already had a century's experience of 'trans-Mediterranean' navigation, which allowed it to escape the enclosure the Muslim world had created in Europe for centuries and to launch out to control the Central and Southern Atlantic.[5] Enrique the Navigator (1394-1460) enabled Portugal to conquer West Africa, supported by many papal bulls which blessed anti-Islamic crusades. Ceuta fell into Christian hands in 1415 and in 1418 the first Afro-Christian diocese was established. In the same year the Portuguese crossed Cape Bojador. In 1420 they occupied the isles of Madeira and their influence extended over the whole of Atlantic Africa.

In the bull *Rex regum* (4 April 1418) Pope Martin V invited European Christians to unite with the Portuguese in their crusade against the Muslims. Thus Portugal acquired a right of control over the Church (the *Padroado*)[6] and at the same time the duty to 'propagate the faith' ('. . . *fidei propagationem et divini cultus augmentum*').[7] Portugal acquired privileges from the bull *Romanus Pontifiex* (8 January 1455) and Spain did likewise in the Canaries and especially in Granada, where through the bull *Provisionis Nostrae* (15 May 1486) it defined the model of colonial Christendom which would be applied in the rest of the world (in Latin America and the Philippines, and also in Africa and Asia by Portugal).

The arrival of the Spaniards in the Caribbean (12 October 1492) and of the Portuguese in Brazil (Cabral arrived in 1500) opened a new horizon to European Christendom. Between 1519 and 1550 the whole Aztec Empire, the Mayas and the Incas, were conquered and evangelised. 30-40 million people (at the highest estimate but at any rate no less than 15 million) accepted Christianity under the domination of Christendom. The mercantile world of the Mediterranean overflowed into the Atlantic. Weapons preceded the gospel and gold and silver were the precious goods, whose acquisition was far more important than the life or death of the natives.

In this violent expansion of Christendom, the aims of Church and State were united.

In the beginning of his *Recodification of the Laws of the Indias* (1681) the King of Spain declared: 'Through his infinite mercy and goodness God our Lord has deigned to give us such a large part of the lordship of this world . . . we have happily succeeded in bringing to the Holy Roman Catholic Church the innumerable peoples and nations who dwell in the Western Indies . . . and others subject to our dominion.'[8]

The first American dioceses were founded in 1504 and 1512 (in Santo Domingo and Puerto Rico) and with them a Church bound up with the ruling State; the ecclesiastical hierarchy was closely linked with the ruling class (who were partly traders and shortly to be traders in negro slaves). There were prophets (like Bartholomew de las Casas) and saints (like Toribio of Mogrovejo, Archbishop of Lima who tried to escape from the system of patronage), but as a rule Christianity remained caught in the toils of Christendom which savagely put down any people who rebelled against oppression.

Portugal, for its part, established contact between the Southern Atlantic and the Indian Ocean and extended its power to India and the Far East. The dioceses of Funchal (1514) in the Madeira Isles, San Salvador (1551) in Brazil, San Salvador (1585) in the Congo, Loanda (1596) in Angola, Goa (1534) in India and Manila (1581) in the Philippines (dependent on Spanish Mexico) extended the Church throughout the world previously violently conquered by soldiers and traders.[9] Iberian mercantilism, which had first conquered commercial routes from the Arabs and afterwards conquered them at Lepanto, was spiritually legitimised by a preaching of the gospel, which in the eyes of the conquered peoples frequently seemed like forcible acceptance of the conqueror's culture.

Witnesses like St Francis Xavier (who lived in Goa from 1542-1545 and died in Sancian in 1552), Francis Ricci (who arrived in Candragiri in 1601) or Roberto de Nobili (in Madure in 1606) demonstrate Christianity in conflict with Christendom. However, Christendom won, at least on the question of the liturgy. By the bull *Omnium sollicitudo* (12 September 1744) Benedict XIV condemned the Indian liturgy. This shows that Roman Christianity had identified with Latin culture and a great struggle would be needed to free the gospel from European culture, the feudal and monarchical system of Christendom.

### 3. THE CAPITALIST EXPANSION OF OTHER FORMS OF CHRISTIANITY

The emancipation of Holland from Spanish rule enabled the emergent capitalist nation to take its place as a new colonial power and propagator of Christianity. In 1602 the Dutch East India Company was founded. Its ends were purely commercial but it also employed missionaries. Years later Guilherme Usselinx founded the West Indies Company with religious aims 'to lead many thousands of people to the light of truth and eternal blessedness'.[10] The 'model' of Christendom appeared again, this time not with Catholics but with Protestants and linked not to mercantilism but to capitalism which was moving towards the industrial revolution.

The Dutch made their presence felt through their companies and their missionaries in Australia (1605), Indochina (they took Solor in 1613); they fought the Portuguese over Angola and they ruled part of Brazil (1630-1654); they took Malacca in 1641 and in 1614 they founded New Amsterdam (which was to become New York). The presence of capitalist traders with their ships and their armies enabled the missionaries to preach and the missionaries for their part legitimised the action of the colonisers and conquerors (the Europeans' 'civilising mission'). Once more the gospel had been absorbed by the 'model' of Christendom. In 1668 Ernest de Welz, a missionary and preacher of Christianity, died in Dutch Guyana.

From the sixteenth century onwards England fought with Spain for the dominion of the Caribbean with its pirates under State orders. In 1655 it occupied Jamaica in the heart of the 'American Mediterranean'. The Church of England was not linked to the State in the same way as the Catholic Church in Spain, but the results were the same. It struggled for dominance with the bourgeois class which came to power with Cromwell. Slowly England displaced Holland in all the seas. In 1639 they were at Madras, in 1661 in Bombay, in 1696 in Calcutta, English colonists arrived in North America in 1620 with the Pilgrim Fathers. It is interesting to note that the Society of New England (the first English missionary society) was founded in 1649, the Society for promoting Christian Knowledge in 1698 to support the missions in India and in 1701 the Society for the Propagation of the Gospel in Foreign Parts (which came to mean something like *Propaganda Fide* for the Catholics). The expansion of the British Empire brought with it the Anglican evangelisation of its colonies.

France was not left out either. It made its presence felt in the empty spaces in the colonisable world: in 1608 Champlain founded Quebec, for a short time the French occupied part of Brazil, and their pirates sailed the Caribbean Sea (which resulted in the occupation of the islands of Santo Domingo, Haiti and many other islands: Guadalupe, Martinica, French Guyana, etc.). In 1643 they occupied the Reunion Islands in Africa, and in 1664 the 'French East India Company' was founded in competition with the British.

But the great expansion of the missions from these three powers (Holland, Britain and France, to which we should add Denmark) took place in the nineteenth century, after the Restoration (of the French monarchy) made possible the explosive growth of European capitalism in its form which succeeded free trade: imperialism (centring round the decade 1870-1880). Geopolitically it was Africa, already bled white since the sixteenth century by slavery, which was the centre of European pillage.[11] In 1787 the Methodists had founded their missionary system. Shortly afterwards the Baptist Missionary Society was founded and then in 1795, the interdenominational London Missionary Society. On the Catholic front the White Fathers were founded by Lavigerie in 1868 and the Lutherans had the Evangelish-lutherische Missionsgesellschaft (1836). Between 1849 and 1856 Livingstone began his journeys, which were continued shortly afterwards by Stanley (1879-1881). This is what brought about the 'carving up' of Africa in Berlin (November 1884-February 1885). The 'body' of Africa was cut up into pieces which the Christian colonising States divided 'rationally'. When the Boers were defeated in 1902, the whole of Africa was one huge colony. Along the railways and roads which transported the wealth extracted from the colonies, the missionaries travelled, justifying once more the power of the rulers of the world. Beside the British and French soldiers, the merchants, the mining companies, the exporters of primary materials came the flourishing Christian missions. Many natives were converted. Becoming a Christian meant ceasing to be African or Asiatic (just as in the sixteenth century the American Indians suffered the same fate). The Christian religion had almost become identified with 'western civilisation'. The model of Christendom linked to the expansion of capitalist imperialism became world-wide. British domination lasted till 1945. Another Anglo-Saxon power was to take its place.

In fact the thirteen British colonies in North America had attained their independence in 1776. They had grown. Their messianic Christianity grew together with the expansion of free trading capitalism and the small landowners in New England. This was a long way from 1649 when the Corporation for the Propagation of the Gospel in New England was founded to convert the Indians. First it was necessary to reach Texas and California. From 1898 onwards a missionary Protestantism appeared in Puerto Rico and Cuba, then in Panama and the Caribbean, the whole of Latin America (after the Congress of Panama in 1916), in Africa, and especially in Pacific Asia. The American

Board of Commissioners for Foreign Missions had been founded in 1810 and the American Bible Society in 1816 and their missionaries crossed the seas.

Thus it appeared that the Christendoms of developed capitalism had universalised Christianity. However, the limitations of this 'missionary spirit' soon became apparent. Although it produced great heroism and even sanctity in many cases, and at the subjective and individual level it was a worthy cause, it was tainted with a fundamental ingenuousness about its ultimate real significance: the 'missionary zeal' of European and North American expansion legitimised, in the name of Christianity, their domination of all the rest of the world: Africa, Asia, Latin America. . . . This is the fundamental ambiguity of the whole modern enterprise of evangelisation. The missions imposed their own culture and Christendom used the churches to guarantee the hegemony of the State and the ruling classes. They imposed a consensus among the colonised people, which allowed oppression to go unchecked.

### 4. MOVEMENTS OF EMANCIPATION AND THE CRISIS OF CHRISTENDOM

Byzantine Christianity was destroyed in the middle of the fifteenth century and at the same time Latino-German medieval Christendom suffered the crisis of passing from feudal decay to the rise of capitalism. From the beginning of the nineteenth century onwards another crisis arose, which will continue well into the twenty-first century. This is the process of the emancipation of the colonies (political and military emancipation) which continues as a struggle for self-determined development (financial, industrial and technological) and the passage from a capitalist to socialist society (a process which has been undertaken by 40 per cent of mankind). The crisis will get worse for Europeans and North American Christendoms. And worse still for the Third World churches, confronted with the process of national emancipation and liberation from dependence on capitalist régimes. This will require the creation of a new 'model' for the Church (perhaps it might be an old 'model'—the earliest one?).

After the emancipation of the United States and Haiti in the eighteenth century, the Spanish and Portuguese colonies became independent during the first quarter of the nineteenth century (with the exception of Cuba and Puerto Rico in 1898). Colonised Asia had to wait till the Second World War to gain its independence (in particular the independent republic of India under Nehru in 1950). Africa's independence came even later (Ghana attained independence with Nkrumah in 1957). This process which is by no means complete presents the churches founded in the Third World in a 'missionary spirit' with a double challenge. They must become separate from the founding churches and then, if possible (as in Latin America), to try to form a national model of Christendom (in relation to the new independent State). This re-establishment of a national Christendom in Third World countries is not possible when Christians are a very small minority (as in Asia), only when they are a majority (as in Zaïre). At any rate this is the end of the age of missions and the beginning of the relative autonomy of the churches in the Third World. Christendom dominated by Europe and the United States (whether Catholic or Protestant, from Spain, Portugal, Holland, Britain, France, Denmark, Belgium or the US) is now confronted by the Third World churches and their growing awareness of the need for Christianity expressed in terms of their own cultures and not a dubious dominating universalism.

Added to this there is a second crisis. The countries dominated by British (now North American) capitalism, are faced with a struggle for liberation from their financial, industrial and technological dependence on the central capitalist countries (Europe, Japan and the US). In the seventeenth century Protestant Christians originated capitalism, and after many crises Catholicism adapted to its ends at the end of the nineteenth century. Today it is difficult to grasp the needs of a post-capitalist society. It requires the abandonment of that model of Christendom and the deposing of the State and the bourgeois ruling class as the propounders of this model. The Third World churches have to seek a new way to evangelise their newly emerging societies.

## 5. TOWARDS A NEW 'MODEL' OF THE CHURCH?

If Christendom was the 'model' in which the hierarchical structure of the Church took its place in political society allied with the system's ruling class, legitimising the State and, vice versa, using the State to enable it to accomplish certain pastoral tasks[12] among its Christian people, this model is no longer viable for two reasons. Either the emancipated State no longer wishes to fulfil this function (as in Asia and the majority of African nations) or the State is no longer capitalist (as in Vietnam or Cuba for example). In both cases the Church must take its place in civil society and begin (without the aid of 'establishment' by the State) to preach the gospel straight. But in its preaching to the whole society it must start with the poor and oppressed, in whatever situation the country happens to be at the moment. It may be in the final throes of capitalist domination (which can last many decades and produce many martyrs, like the Archbishop of El Salvador, Mons. Oscar Arnulfo Romero). It may be actually engaged in the struggle for liberation. It may be in a period when an ill-conceived 'democratic centralism' exhorts its people to fight to strengthen democracy in socialist countries. The Church must be a people's Church; today in the Third World it must stand with the people. This siding with the oppressed requires a new 'model' of the Church, or perhaps a return to the model that existed before the creation of Christendom.

This is why choosing the poor, preaching the gospel from local communities, the presence of Christians in the fight for liberation (as in Nicaragua), the struggle for human rights, and the witnesses of countless Christian martyrs are signs of change, of the birth in the Church of a new 'model' a new way of seeing the relationship between the Church and the world, the hierarchy and the State, the Christian faith and history.

The Church's position will be different in different situations, in the main capitalist countries, the dependent capitalist countries, developed socialist countries, etc. It will not be the same in Poland where Christian workers are fighting to democratise the socialist system in the name of their faith, as in El Salvador where Christian workers and peasants are fighting to free their country from capitalism itself. In both cases the Church, if it is *with the people* and supporting the people's cause and not that of the political society or the ruling classes, must have as its model a 'people's Church'. The model of Christendom must be superseded, looking sometimes to the past and sometimes to the future. Nothing in history is perfect, although some acts are more paradigmatic than others.

That is why when Jesus was asked whether he was the Messiah or was the Messiah still to come, he replied, 'The poor have the gospel preached to them'. If the Church preaches the gospel to the poor from among the poor, it will be a 'Church of the poor'—as John XXIII liked to call it—a *people's Church*. The present contradiction in the Church is the contradiction between the two models: one representing the power of the Church allied to the rich States and ruling classes, the other the Church siding with the oppressed and fighting for the freedom of the poor countries. The contradiction between capitalism and socialism is also a contradiction in the Church. A Church on the model of a 'people's Church' is the one which has the hope of fulfilling its mission, preaching the gospel, growing, proceeding towards the Parousia in a future egalitarian society, without rich and poor countries, even though new forms of oppression may arise to be combated in their turn.

The crisis of Christendom offers a great opportunity to Christian creativity. Christendom is dying. Let us be glad because this will enable Christianity to grow.

*Translated by Dinah Livingstone*

## Notes

1. See *Werke* (Jena 1909) VIII p. 319; VII pp. 61ff.

2. 'Eine verkehrte Welt' (see Pap., p. 129).

3. See vol. 1, chap. 3 of our *Historia General de la Iglesia en America Latina* (due shortly from Sigueme, Salamanca; Orbis Books, New York; Vozes, Petrópolis). Commissioned by CEHILA. And see the bibliography therein.

4. This is the subject of part 1, vol. 1 of the work cited in note 3.

5. See Pierre Chanu *Conquête et exploitation des nouveaux mondes* (Paris 1977).

6. '. . . jus patronatus et praesentandi personas idoneas ad quaecumque ecclesiae et ecclesiastica . . .' (*Bullar. Portug.* I p. 99).

7. *Ibid.* p. 31.

8. Book 1, para. 1 law 1.

9. See Kenneth Scott Latourette *A History of the Expansion of Christianity* (Grand Rapids 1976) III, V, VI and VII.

10. C. Ligtenberg Willem Usselinx (Utrecht 1913) p. 69 (quoting Klaus van der Grijp).

11. L. H. Gann and Peter Duignan *Colonialism in Africa* (1870-1960 Cambridge) I-II, 1969-1970. See especially chap. 14: 'Missionary and humanitarian aspects of Imperialism' (I pp. 462ff.).

12. See para. 1 of this article.

# PART III

Clodovis Boff

# The Nature of Basic
# Christian Communities

IN THIS brief account of the Basic Christian Communities (or 'Basic Communities', or 'Basic Ecclesial Communities', as they are also sometimes known—henceforth abbreviated to BC), I propose first to describe their structure, then examine their ecclesiology and finally their theological methodology.

## 1. DESCRIPTION

This section is intended mainly for those who are unable to gain first- or second-hand knowledge of the BC's, and sets out to describe what they are, what they are made up of, how they function, what they do and what they feel like.

### (a) What they are

BC's are made up of small groups of an average of ten people; it is most usually a number of these groups—generally ten—grouped in one area, usually one parish, that is known as a BC. A large parish may encompass more than one BC—five, six, or more. But the small groups themselves are also sometimes referred to as BC's. This varies with the conditions of the area; so where population density is low, one group will be a BC. It also depends on the way people use the term: some automatically use it to describe a small group and some a group of these groups; there is no consistency in this. But normally the structure goes from small group to BC to parish. This shows that the BC is not, in principle, incompatible with the parish and with existing church structures in general. For its part, the small group can have different aspects and names: evangelising group, bible-study group, reflective group, prayer group, etc.

### (b) What they are made up of

The overwhelming majority of members of the BC's are poor people. They come from the lowest strata of society, the peasants and the workers—those who suffer. This is not principally a religious but a social fact: evidence shows it to be so. In fact, the BC's have till now only flourished in the two areas where the poor live: the country districts and the peripheries of the big cities. Is this why the word 'basic' is applied to them? Partly so. In other Latin American countries they are called 'popular' rather than 'basic'—with the same social implication. These are the people for whom the gospel can ring out for what it is: the Good News of the kingdom, of total liberation. But the BC's also include some members from the middle and even the upper classes, generally pastoral workers, responsible for a specific sector or task within the community. These are lay people who have committed themselves to the cause of the poor for the sake of 'liberating evangelisation'.

### (c) How they arise

The underlying reason why dispersed and oppressed people come together in an *ekklesia* can be either religious or social. If it is the former, it can have various causes and motives: the need to keep faith alive among people who have no priest; the need to develop a more personal and committed form of faith; the simple suggestion from a priest, religious or lay person that a BC be formed; the multiplication of groups by a sort of fissiparous process; the birth of new groups thanks to the evidence of pastoral efficacity of existing ones; the 'export' of the idea via a pastor transferred from one district to another, or a lay person who has moved; the increasing support and insistent recommendation of the hierarchies of most Latin American countries of this type of organisation, etc. In these cases, BC's are nearly always formed from the existing nucleus of some existing religious group—confraternity, etc.—or common-interest grouping—bible-study circles, chaplaincies, traditional associations, etc.). But BC's also come into being as a result of social concerns: the threat of slum clearance, the danger of dispossession, the need to press for improvements in a neighbourhood, preparation for a strike, etc. Once brought into being in this way, the group feels the need for regular meetings for prayer or reflection on its problems in the light of its common faith, particularly when there is a pastoral worker involved in these activities.

### (d) How they work

The basic group usually meets once a week, in a set place, usually a family house, but it might be any room available, in a chapel or simply in the shade of a tree. And what do they do? They pray, they listen to the Word of God, and they discuss problems affecting their lives. Prayer, Word, Life: these are the three elements common to every meeting. They are inter-related: one prays because of the joys or sorrows of life—life which is discussed in the light of the Word of the gospel. Naturally, there is always an 'animator' in the group, whose function is to lead in prayer, and to share out the readings and chair the discussion. Besides him or her, other functions emerge more or less spontaneously according to the needs of the moment: people take charge of the sick, take up a collection, lead the singing and the reading, and so on. These are lay ministers at the most basic level.

### (e) What they do

The BC's are communities whose purpose includes action. The direction in which they are orientated is towards specific commitment to their local community and to society at large. This is why a BC may undertake a variety of activities: religious (catechesis, bible-study, prayer weeks, etc.) and social (improvements in the neighbourhood, collective works, teaching the illiterate to read, political and legal education, creation and strengthening of trade unions, participation in party political activities, etc.). The type and degree of commitment in these fields will depend on the social character of the BC in question and the stage of development or maturity it has reached.

### (f) What they are like

What is the spirit, style or manner of being of the BC's? How can one describe their spiritual characteristics?

In the first place, what impresses is their *evangelism*—being evangelical in the sense of giving off a feeling of joy, hope and freedom. The atmosphere of a BC is one of brotherhood and general benevolence. One is welcomed, accepted and appreciated. Above all, a BC is a community that radiates joy, the joy of simple, poor people, without formality or hidden aspects; a sincere, spontaneous joy that comes straight from the heart and goes direct to the heart. The beauty of this joy is that it arises in the midst of the hardest of conditions of life, often indeed in the midst of tragedy. This evangelical joy expresses the transcendence of the spirit, rising above the most oppressive social situations—a special gift of the Holy Spirit. The atmosphere in a BC is full of human worth and greatness of heart, but never the ingenuous happiness of those who know nothing of the contradictions and hardships of life. No, it goes with a fairly critical outlook on reality, a very sharp class feeling, and an extremely committed and dangerous struggle, all without a trace of bitterness or resentment. Life's hardships and brutal challenges are as it were sublimated in this atmosphere of pure evangelical existence. It is this spirit that distinguishes the 'community' member of a BC from any other political militant of the Left on one hand, and from the typical bourgeois Christian on the other. In the BC's, I really think one experiences the quintessence of the gospel in its innermost and truest sense.

A second spiritual characteristic of the BC's is their expression of the idea of *community*. Sharing is the general norm: of faith, of prayer, of the Word, of the problems of life and their solutions, of material goods, of physical help and even of faults. It is of the utmost importance that everyone in a BC participates to excess, that everyone speaks, puts forward an opinion, asks a favour, makes a suggestion, offers a commentary on the gospel. This is a real exercise in participatory democracy. It is what is responsible for developing their critical, ecclesial and social sense.

The third characteristic of the BC's is their *militancy*. They are groups of people who act, who commit themselves. The whole dynamic of the BC's is towards action, and towards action for liberation in particular. This can go from mere struggle for survival to attempts at changing the social (political) structure of society. What is admirable is to see the generosity and courage with which simple, often illiterate people face the challenges of their lives and of the society they live in. They show that even when pushed under, virtually suffocated by the burdens forced on them, the oppressed poor still have reserves of fight, of life, of joy.

### 2. ECCLESIOLOGY

The image of the Church found in the BC's has two basic aspects: one intra-ecclesial and the other extra-ecclesial. The BC's are communities of faith and communities of charity; they are prayer groups and action groups. This is how Puebla saw them and how John-Paul II addressed them in his message to the BC's of Brazil. So they possess both an ecclesial and a secular dimension. They exist in the sphere of the Church (as a cellular church) and in the domain of society (as grass-roots communities).

Three ecclesiological aspects characteristic of BC's can be mentioned here: they are communities of the poor, communities of the Word, and communities in the people's

E

Church. Poor, Word, People—these define the ecclesiological character of the BC's. But as they have one face turned inward (faith) and another outward (charity), these aspects go in pairs: poor/believers, Word/life, people's Church/caring society. These are the points I propose to develop.

### (a) Poor/believers

The first constituent of a BC is that people from the popular classes, who are both religious and poor, come together in the name of faith.

*Poor people*. The BC's put into practice the original meaning of the gospel: the poor, the humble and the outcasts of society come and take their place in a church. They sit at the table of God and his Word. They form a community, they constitute a church of the blessed (through grace).

*Religious people*. The members of the BC's are drawn from amongst the great mass of those who have been baptised. They find their basic inspiration in the religion of the people, the faith of the People of God. So they find no conflict between the religion of the people and the faith of the Church. In the BC's, the gospel becomes flesh and blood, the life and wisdom of the people. On the other hand, popular religion is educated, elevated and evangelised in the BC's, redeemed, one might say, through the power of its symbols and the value of its practices.

This raises a problem: how does the group faith of the BC's relate to the elementary faith of the religious masses? The BC's act as a sort of mediating influence, welcoming the richness of popular religion and returning it reinvigorated and as it were re-processed. The BC's do not claim to be a church for minorities, of the élite. They want to remain rooted in the Christian masses, feeding on their vital energy and feeding them with the sap of the gospel.

### (b) Word/life

*Word*. The community takes shape as such around the Word, particularly the words of the gospel, not primarily round the person of a priest. Of course, they have leaders and these may be priests, but if they are, they place themselves on the same level as the rest of the community, as hearers of the liberating Word and sharers in the common life and struggle.

*Life*. The reading of the Word is always actualised, applied to life situations, confronted with reality: basic needs, sufferings, rights, struggle. The people look to the Word for life in its fullness—liberation and salvation indissolubly blended.

This raises another problem, and a serious one: the relationship between BC's and other popular movements or groups, such as civil rights associations, trade unions and political parties. This relationship depends mainly on social conditions. Where there are no adequate civil organisations already in existence, the BC's make up for the lack, even in non-religious affairs: cultural (courses of literacy, health education, legal instruction, and so on), political (following up various claims, demonstrations, creation of independent party committees, etc.), or economic (community savings and insurance schemes, financial assistance to trade unions, organisation of cooperatives . . .). But where there are already adequate secular organisations in existence, the BC's act as training grounds for leaders and active members, as a critical force and support group. Whatever the case, the BC's are always particularly careful to maintain their separate identity, their specific difference. And when circumstances force them into the temporal arena, as into politics, they always do so impelled and inspired by the evangelical principle and because there is no one else to do so. In other cases, individual members, not the BC's as social groups, personally, legitimately and responsibly take on temporal tasks. Cases where BC's have transformed themselves into purely secular organs are the very rare exception, though a valuable warning nonetheless.

### (c) People's church/caring society

*People's church.* By virtue of their number and their originality, the BC's constitute an ecclesial phenomenon of the greatest significance. Social studies of the institutional church agree in recognising in the popular classes, particularly through the BC's, the new social base of the Church in Latin America. They are determining the general direction and historical course of the Church on this continent. This in no way implies a new Church, still less one in opposition to what is called the institutional Church. It is rather the Church of Jesus itself being converted and restructured on the basis of the poor people, becoming more religious through the work of the BC's. So doctrinal formulation, liturgical expression and the organisation of religious structures are all becoming increasingly popular. Pastors themselves are changing through contact with the BC's, becoming simpler, better listeners, poorer: more evangelical, in short—a fact which was recognised at Puebla and impressed the pope on his visit to Brazil.

*Caring society.* The BC's are not only giving the institution of the Church a new look, they are doing the same to society at large. Within them, a new way of living together is being tried out, in which each individual is the centre of the educative and decision-making processes at all levels. So in terms of historical progress, one might say that the BC's have a proleptic, anticipatory function. But the BC's contribute to the emergence of a new society not only through their own internal practice. They do so more directly in the social, i.e., the political, sphere. Here their members are something more than historical agents in the general sense that everyone is; they are qualified agents, bearers of the ferment of the gospel to the world.

The major question posed now is this: that a new Church and a new society each stands in need of the other.

### 3. THEOLOGICAL METHOD

Like everything else in the Church: language, worship and organisation, so theological practice has both influenced the BC's and been modified under their influence. This influence has been felt both on the level of the external conditions in which theology is practised and on the level of the internal conditions or rules of theological practice.

### (a) External conditions

There are two conditions that can be specially singled out as significant for theological practice in the light of the BC's: 'collectivity' and 'organicity'. In the BC's, theological practice is both communal and organic.

*Theology as collective practice.* The subject of theology—the BC's have discovered—is the Church. If the faith belongs to all, its deepening, in the form of theological reflection, should also be for all. So the whole of a BC reflects on its faith and enriches it. No *one* theologises for any *one* else, but all theologise for all. In this way, a BC becomes a sort of 'collective theologian'. In Latin America, it is no longer understood how anyone, called 'a theologian', can go to a community in order to instruct it, direct it or think for it. Furthermore, the collective elaboration of faith is done through the various forms of expression and communication of the community itself, itself the subject of its theology. Instead of classical exposition, it plunges into open discussion, group debate, dramatisation, stories, poems, music, celebration, and so forth.

*Theology as organic practice.* Collective theology does not dispense with the professional theologian. On the contrary: it places him back in the theologising community, where his specific function becomes that of helping the community to think its faith seriously, that is, critically and articulately. If he or she is to do this, the theologian must be organically linked to the community as a lively and active member of it, with the particular responsibility of leading collective reflection on faith, since this is what he/she is trained to do.

### (b) Internal conditions

Let us now look at the various moments of the process of this collective and organic theology: analysis of reality, confrontation of reality with the Word of God, directives for action.

In the first place, the reflection of the BC's always starts from reality, from questions raised by the members of the community. There is no theologising from academic questions, or those in vogue. On this level, the community is helped by some 'organic intellectual' (Gramsci) such as a social scientist, and in the absence of such, by its own professional theologian. This is what the methodology of theology in Latin America calls 'socio-analytical meditation'.

Then, the social situation analysed is compared with the Word of God. Here, there are two 'sub-moments' to consider. First, they try to understand the meaning of the text, and here the services of the theologian, or an exegete, are most helpful. Second, on the basis of the first, or textual, meaning, they go on to find an actual, or 'actualised', meaning, relating to the situation under discussion. Here the community naturally works collectively. The methodological approach that ensures the proper process of this operation is called 'hermeneutic meditation'.

Finally, they return to the present situation, but now in the light of the indications thrown up by the confrontation between the situation analysed and the gospel reflected on. This is 'practical meditation' (pastoral or political). So it will be seen that the process of reflecting on faith, that is the theology of the groups, is wholly inspired by a practical purpose: *agape*. This is where theology reaches its term, only to begin again at once, as life begins again.[1]

*Translated by Paul Burns*

*Note*

1. An epistemological discussion of this method and its origin can be found in my *Teologia e Prática* (Petrópolis 1978). There is a Spanish translation and it is being translated into Italian and German.

Tshishiku Tshibangu

# What Counts as the Full Christian Maturity of a Young Church— A reflection on the basis of the development of the African Church

THE MATURING of the concept of the Church, combined with the development of missiology, have resulted in certain ecclesiological as well as missiological positions that were expressed by the supreme magisterium of the Church at Vatican II. This outlined the developmental stages a church that begins by being a 'mission church' goes through on the way to becoming a fully constituted church.

The Council determined that a young church must establish itself in such a way that it is in a position to do all it reasonably can to provide for the necessities of life and effective action. The chief things this implies and entails are as follows: that the Christian spirit should have taken deep root amongst the people; that there should be a solid body of dependable layfolk to embody and express the Christian spirit in the diverse institutions of social life and to radiate Christ and actively spread the gospel; and that there should be enough sacred ministers to ensure the implantation and continued growth of the Church. What this latter means in particular is that there should be enough priests, deacons, catechists and religious with a contemplative as well as an active calling.[1]

A whole chapter of the Decree *Ad gentes* spells it out that the implantation of a young church as a 'local church' can be deemed to have reached a significant turning point when the Christian community enjoys a certain stability and solidity as a result of having been rooted in the social life and made a profound adaptation to local culture.

What guarantees these features are the following elements:

at the human level, the presence of a certain minimum staff of priests, religious and local layfolk;
at the level of ministries, the availability of ministries and all other institutions necessary for the life of the People of God and its development under the guidance of a local episcopate. The Council adds that the elaboration of an appropriate juridical order may be necessary for the support of these ministries;[2]
at the material level, the assurance of a minimum material support;

at the doctrinal level, the maturity of a young church as evidenced by its capacity to make its own specific and solid contribution to theological development.[3]

It is against the background of the Council's definition of the characteristics of a local church and of the conditions for the full maturity of a young church that there has been a great deal of discussion in Africa about the effective conditions for the constitution and development of young churches in Africa as 'local churches'. The characteristics and conditions outlined by the Council were inevitably global and general in definition, and so African Christians and theologians have wanted to establish a few main criteria for ascertaining when a church that begins by being a mission church comes into being as a local church.

## 1. THE ESSENTIAL BASIS FOR THE CONSTITUTION OF A LOCAL CHURCH

This consists in the living existence of a Christian community that has sprung from evangelisation.

Now Fr Meinrad Hebga, a Jesuit from Cameroon, has recently published an analytical article on this subject, under the title 'The Personality of a Local Church: The Sociological and Ecclesiological Criteria of its Emergence'.[4] Fr Hebga begins by making some justifiable criticisms of certain criteria which he maintains are 'ambiguous', such as that which refers to a given number of Christians in the locality, or that which is based on some Christians in the community having been there for a minimum period of time, or that which relates to a 'financial viability' to be duly fixed. He then goes on to maintain that the fundamental basis for the constitution of a church is simply the presence of enough Christians to make a coherent and solid group. The sole condition is that such an assembly of Christians has been endowed, as the first churches were endowed by the apostles, with the structure necessary for the ordinary practice of the Christian life, in particular permanent ministers of the Word and the Eucharist and a minimum framework of organisation and evangelical government.[5] That is one consideration. We should also take into account the fact that becoming a Christian is a personal act which each Christian and each generation live through themselves and have to do integrally. The fact that a Christian community is young does not prevent it from constituting a real part of the Church of Christ. This was inevitably the case for all the first Christian communities, beginning with those that were born during the very lifetime of the apostles.

Moreover, the financial point of view may well constitute a condition of exercise that is of no mean practical importance. The concern to ensure the financial viability of African or Asian local churches has, nevertheless, often retarded their evangelical maturity.[6] At the same time, it is a condition that is worth examining more closely.

## 2. MATERIAL CONDITIONS OF THE FUNCTIONING OF ORGANS OF A CHURCH AND OF THE EXERCISE OF SOCIAL CHARITY

It is a fact that Christian communities have expanded in our day, that the organs of the Church have become ever more complex, and that more and more urgent calls have been made upon the charity of Christians. In these circumstances it is true that the financial aspect and material means in general have become more and more important. We should, however, note in the first place that all these considerations are relevant only to good administrative and structural functioning and cannot be taken to impose a constitutive requirement.

The young churches, as the Council acknowledged, are often enough very poor at the material level.[7] Those in charge of these churches are only too aware of this fact. It can be agreed that 'financial viability' does not of itself lead to a condition *sine qua non*, and yet, practically speaking, the great concern is to try to supply them with these means in order to enable them to do the essential things by themselves in the interests of the continuity, stability and solidity of these young churches.

The perspective adopted in the Decree *Ad gentes* is not very satisfactory for those in charge of the young churches. The Council is effectively content to recommend the old and richer churches to continue to be generous and to help the young churches with gifts and other contributions.[8] The old churches should indeed continue to give material help, but the real effort should be directed towards finding the best possible means to make the young churches really independent.

This is where the real discussion and even tension in the exchanges between those in charge of the young and old churches respectively lie: the young churches tend more and more to say that they wish to receive only occasional and circumstantial help, and, further, help calculated to provide the material infrastructure and human structures for self-help.

### 3. INDIGENOUS ECCLESIAL EXPRESSIONS

A Christian community that has recently been baptised and has assimilated and taken into itself the message of the gospel manifests this by its religious way of thinking, that is to say, by its capacity for theological reflection, as also, in a living manner, by its form of liturgical prayer and its spirituality. What is more, the community is more aware of local needs and so is led to make a better adaptation of existing ecclesial ministries, or even to devise new ones. And so far as catechesis goes, the deeper assimilation and acculturation of the Christian message brings in its wake catechetical forms which cease being pure translations of the catechisms imported directly from old Christendom and become relevant to the people for whom they are meant.

### (a) At the theological level

The young churches take seriously the desire expressed in the Decree *Ad gentes* to have active theological research promoted in their midst: 'A theological reflection, by which the facts and words revealed by God are submitted to a new scrutiny in the light of the tradition of the universal Church should be encouraged in every distinct socio-cultural territory.'[9]

By way of a first phase an evolution has taken place at the level of principle—from a theology of 'adaptation' to the legitimation of a process of 'indigenous elaboration' of Christian theology.[10] In Africa the debates about the principle of a so-called African theology have gone on for nearly twenty years.

The churches in Africa as well as in the Third World generally have now got to the stage of organising theological research effectively. This is why, at the end of a meeting held at Dar-es-Salaam, Tanzania, in August 1976, an Ecumenical Association of Theologians of the Third World was created, comprising theologians from Asia, Latin America and Africa.[11] And on 20 December 1977 the Ecumenical Association of African Theologians was formed at Accra, Ghana.[12] This represents a significant stage in the conscious construction of non-western churches.[13]

### (b) At the liturgical level

Throughout Africa efforts are being made to Africanise the expression of liturgical rites. It is not merely a matter of praying in African languages or of singing to African rhythms; African symbolism permeates the whole range of religious expression. A distinctive set of African rites is even coming into being bit by bit. This is the way in which there is already talk of a 'Mass in the Zaïrian rite' or of a 'Cameroon Mass'. So far, however, these elements of African rites do not yet touch the essential lines and development of the Roman Rite. What does the future hold in store? We cannot foresee this entirely. We should in this connection just bear in mind the criterion of which Pope John-Paul II recently reminded the African bishops: 'A great enrichment is possible in the domain of sacred gestures and the liturgy, provided only that the significance of the Christian rite is properly preserved and that the universal, catholic aspect of the Church remains clearly apparent . . . in union with the other local churches and in agreement with the Holy See.'[14]

### (c) At the level of spirituality

Every people possesses its own traditional principles of the spiritual life. The peoples of Africa, carried along as they are by strictly organised religions and directed as they are by a distinct philosophy of the world, have their own spiritual experience. The Christian faith has come to take up and animate this spiritual experience. It is important to enable this to develop and flourish after it has been marked with the Christian seal which purifies and raises it up. This goes for inner spiritual experience in general. So far as the organised exterior forms of spiritual life are concerned, the process of evangelisation has been accompanied by the installation of forms and structures of spirituality imported ready-made from elsewhere. The most notable examples are those inspired by the various currents of spirituality of the religious congregations and secular institutes born in the West.

It is very important indeed for the renewal and acculturation of the personal and community forms of prayer, liturgy and spirituality to incorporate the language of prayer and the resources of deep spiritual experience of Africa.

The situation at present is that, after a first period of the flowering of vocations, Africans lived through a fairly widespread crisis during the Fifties and Sixties. Today the imported forms of contemplative life in Africa are evaluated for their prayer content, the adequacy of their style of life for the realisation of the traditional religious vows and their suitability to local life.[15] We hope that the forthcoming publication, in the framework of the Ecumenical Association of African Theologians, of a periodical of 'African spirituality' will give a welcome fillip to reflection on this very important aspect of Christian life.[16]

### (d) At the level of ministries

A great deal of thought is being given in all churches to the question of introducing new ministries calculated to respond to the concrete needs of the Christian community and Christian society. Research is particularly concerned with the organisation of non-ordained ministries.[17]

### (e) At the level of catechesis

It is at this level that the distinctive personality of the African churches is beginning to assert itself. We have already mentioned the fact that there has been a shift from the simple adoption of the catechisms of European dioceses brought in by the missionaries and merely translated to the elaboration of new catechisms meant to be relevant to the questions and needs of African Christianity. The principles governing the elaboration of these catechisms were declared by the bishops of Africa in the Declaration on Catechesis published at the end of the Third Synod of Bishops in Rome in 1974.[18]

## 4. DISCIPLINARY AND JURIDICAL ORGANISATION

It is quite normal that as soon as a Christian community lives and develops in any given and differentiated socio-cultural space it should tend to have its own distinctive administrative and juridical organisation. This is a principle. Will the churches of Africa, founded as they were by western missionaries from the so-called 'Latin' church, always be content to depend, without modification, on the Roman ecclesiastical law, or will they evolve towards their own distinctive juridical organisation?

In any case more and more people in Africa have seized upon the opportunity of the current revision of the Code of Canon Law and of the elaboration of a Fundamental Law of the Church (*Lex fundamentalis Ecclesiae*) to express the wish that room should be left for a distinctive application of fundamental principles to local circumstances in the light of different historical and cultural situations, over and above the general principles of ecclesiastical organisation based on the gospel and on the Christian tradition valid everywhere. Such a development can be nothing but desirable, provided only that at the bottom of all this the churches of Africa keep from their origin in the West their ties of filiation and quite particular relationship with Latin church organisation. The future will tell what is in store.[19]

What is clear is that at this moment African Christians are so conscious of representing a different sort of ecclesiastical world that there has been considerable talk over several years of a general meditation and reflection on the Church in Africa and its specific problems, a reflection in depth to be conducted in the course of an 'African Council' or at least an 'African Synod' to be presided over by the pope of Rome.[20] This tells us a great deal about the will that African Christians have to take their own responsibility for problems of the Church that are specific to them.

## 5. A LEADERSHIP AWARE OF WHAT IS AT STAKE

What we have tried to do above is to analyse various criteria by which we could recognise the coming to maturity and authenticity of the young churches.

Now the single most important factor in this process of maturing is the quality and value of the apostolic agents in the young churches. Amongst them the essential condition is the capital and irreplaceable rôle of those in charge of the churches. The young churches will come into their own through the action of animators and true leaders who are aware of their responsibility and who have to know that they are called to be the creative shapers of the young local churches of today, on the model of the apostles and the first Fathers of the Church who founded the first Christian churches.[21]

*Translated by John Maxwell*

*Notes*

1. See the Decree *Ad gentes* § 15.
2. *Ibid.*, § 19.
3. *Ibid.*, § 22.
4. M. Hebga 'Personnalité de l'Eglise particulière: critères sociologiques et ecclésiologiques de son émergence' *Bulletin de Theologie Africaine* 3 (1980) 23-34.
5. *Ibid.*, 28.

6. *Ibid.*, 27.

7. Decree *Ad gentes* § 19.

8. *Ibid.* ; '. . . these mission churches are often to be found in the poorest parts of the world and they usually suffer from a serious lack of priests and material support. As a result their absolute need is that the pursuit of the missionary activity of the whole Church ensures them the aid above all to promote the growth of the local church and the maturing of Christian life' § 19.

9. *Ibid.*, § 22.

10. See A. M. Ngindu 'La Théologie africaine. De la polémique à l'irénisme critique' *Bulletin de Théologie Africaine* 1 (1979) 69-98.

11. The purpose of the research undertaken is defined as follows in the *Manifesto of Ecumenical Dialogue of the Theologians of the Third World*: 'The theologies of Europe and North America are still dominant in our churches. . . . They have to be understood as having emerged from the particular situations of these countries and must not, therefore, be adopted without criticism or without an opportunity on our part to question their relevance in the context of our own countries.' See *The Emergent Gospel. Theology from the Underside of History* (New York 1977). For the details of the origins of the Association of the Theologians of the Third World see O. K. Bimwenyi 'Déplacements. A l'origine de l'Association Oecumenique de Théologiens du Tiers-Monde' *Bulletin de Théologie Africaine* 3 (1980) 41-53.

12. The aims of the Association are defined as follows: 'to promote and develop an African theology; to encourage and strengthen cooperation between theologians of different languages, regions and Christian confessions in Africa; to favour the exchange of theological publications and experiences in Africa; to help the churches in Africa to live their Christian experience according to their socio-historic genius; to stimulate the spirit of theological research in Africa; to facilitate ecumenical rapprochement and dialogue and to link up work done by African Christian theologians of the Catholic, Protestant or Orthodox traditions or belonging to the independent churches.' See *Bulletin de Théologie Africaine* (1979) 299.

13. The action programme of the Ecumenical Association of African Theologians has just been worked out and formulated on the occasion of the first general meeting of the Association which was held from 24-28 September 1980, in Yaounde in Cameroon. The proceedings of this meeting are due to be published shortly.

14. John-Paul II *Discours aux Evêques du Zaïre*, on 3 May 1980. See *Le Pape chez nous* (Kinshasa 1980). Some theologians are already raising squarely the question of the matter of the Eucharist: see, for example, Uzuku 'Les Traditions élémentaires africaines et l'Eucharistie' in *Bulletin de Théologie Africaine* 4 (1980).

15. See A. Shorter *African Christian Spirituality* (London 1978); *Christianity in Independent Africa* (London 1978).

16. The proposed contents of this publication include: expositions of problems of spirituality; accounts of spiritual experience; reports of spiritual testimonies.

17. See on this subject the proceedings of the *Huitième Semaine Théologique de Kinshasa* which had as its theme 'Ministries and Services in the Church' (23-28 July 1975), Faculté de Théologie Catholique de Kinshasa, 1979.

18. See *Documentation Catholique* (1974).

19. The target for the first period is to secure 'a larger extent and a greater autonomy of local legislation'. Later, no doubt, there will be serious question of *a canon law elaborated for Africa*. See in this regard the interesting article of G. Thils 'La Révision du droit canonique et les problèmes ecclésiologiques qu'elle rencontre' *Revue Theologique de Louvain* 9 (1978) 329-341.

20. Address of the bishops of Zaïre to Pope John-Paul II at Kinshasa on 3 May 1980.

21. Cardinal Malula *L'Eveque africain, aujourd'hui et demain* (Kinshasa 1980).

Jacques van Nieuwenhove

# Implications of Puebla for the Whole Church

PUEBLA HAS commonly been seen and interpreted in the light of what it means for the present and future of the Church in Latin America. Only a few European commentators have dealt with it directly from the angle of its repercussions on the Church as a whole, and particularly on western Christianity.[1]

This article therefore deals with an area which is still largely unexplored. Moreover, Puebla by itself already covers such a vast range of topics that one can treat only some of its most important aspects. The content of this article is therefore limited to some provisional and general observations on a subject which really deserves a much broader treatment.

Any study of the possible, desirable or expected effects which Puebla may have on the Church at large will have to take into account the differences in the religious, cultural, social and political character of the churches outside Latin America. The pastoral-theological project of Puebla cannot possibly have the same effects in the same way and to the same extent in the churches of Africa, Asia, Europe and North America with all their varied groupings. In order to avoid controversial extrapolations I am not going into definite questions about the interpretation and applicability of Puebla with regard to other local churches and situations.

I cannot even explain why I think that Puebla will and should have such wider consequences. In this connection V. Cosmao maintains that Puebla is a pioneering event which projects the image of the Roman Catholic Church of the future.[2] He holds this view not so much because the Latin American bishops represent 43 per cent of all Catholics in the present world but because they are the spokesmen of a Church which is developing in an exemplary fashion vital forces contained in the gospel and thus plays a stimulating, critical, corrective and even challenging part in the whole Church. But a detailed discussion of this prognosis is beyond the scope of this article and will not be undertaken here.

I shall first try to indicate how Puebla should be interpreted and which focal issues of its pastoral theology may be said to contain a real message for the whole Church. After that I shall turn my attention to some aspects of this message, particularly concentrating on the solidarity between the Church and the Latin American 'people', and finally highlight some points of what Puebla says about the liberating *diakonia*.

## 1. WHERE DOES PUEBLA SHOW THE CORE OF ITS ORIGINALITY?

An immense amount has been published on the significance of the Puebla event. Both Latin American and European commentators have debated which points of the conference will have the greatest impact on the daily direction and faithfulness of the local church communities. And here the discussions on the interpretation of the text of the final conclusions play an important part. In his analysis J. C. Scannone has shown that there are not only differences but even mutual contradictions in the interpretations of these theological and pastoral conclusions given by church authorities and theologians.[3]

This conflict of interpretation concerns first of all the question of how to reconcile the diverging visions of the document with each other, and, beyond this, the matter of the basic intent and identity of the whole evangelisation project of Puebla.

Many have interpreted Puebla as a confrontation between liberation theology with its pastoral implications, based on the spirit and the letter of Medellín, and an alternative theology of communion and participation which not only sought to correct and modify this liberation movement but radically to oppose it.

This approach to the conference is useful because it accentuates not only Puebla's social criticism but also its theology of integral liberation and the prophetic mission of the Church. It also manages to expose not only the tensions and contradictions between the theology of the bishops and that of the theologians, but also the internal tensions existing within the episcopal college. The danger here is that this attitude reduces the message of Puebla to only one of its essential components.

There is another way of looking at Puebla. The final conclusions show throughout a pastoral-theological intent which many see as the dominating preoccupation of Puebla. This is the view that the truly essential mission of the Church is to evangelise Latin American culture and to strengthen the pastoral dialogue with the 'people', with their sense of dignity, their religious attitudes, expectations and rights.

This would imply that Puebla concentrated on the fact that Latin America is becoming increasingly aware of its cultural, social and political identity and of the special character of its own individual history where the mission and the Church are concerned.

It also means that the magisterium tried to find ways of fitting in with the faith as experienced by the Christian communities, particularly the ordinary people, so that it can reflect more profoundly and more explicitly than in Medellín upon the theological and spiritual identity of the Church's life in community and pastoral praxis. Among other things this means that the bishops took a more independent stance with regard to western post-conciliar theology and the praxis of the European and North American churches and wanted to examine the new Latin American thinking in theology in the light of the Spirit as manifested in the Christian awareness on the broader base of the local churches.

## 2. PUEBLA'S MEANING FOR THE WHOLE CHURCH

Puebla was very well aware of the world-wide significance of Latin American Christianity. It wanted to reinforce its missionary contribution to the Church at large because Christians of this sub-continent 'have something original and important to offer to all: their sense of salvation and liberation, the richness of their people's religiosity, the experience of their basic communities, their flourishing diversity of ministries, and their hope and joy rooted in the faith'.[4] These ways of living the faith and of pastoral renewal thus convey a message to the Church at large. Moreover, Puebla is also aware of the fact that the underdevelopment and oppression which beset Latin America as part of the Third World are a world problem, and not merely a regional one. Its analysis of society and the world-situation finds expression in its sharp protest against cultures and ideologies imported from the West and in the decision to promote the urgent demands of the Third World as embodied in Latin America.

This point is emphasised in its demand for international cooperation wherever human rights, particularly among the weak and the exploited throughout the world, are threatened and violated. On this point Puebla has thrown out a real challenge, and one still wonders how Christians of the industrialised countries will meet this criticism and respond to this pressing invitation to cooperate.

In Puebla the Latin American bishops asked themselves how a Church could become a Church for the poor and with the poor; how such a Church could and should show that it accepts its responsibilities in the struggle for justice, and what this conversion to the poor implied in the way of self-criticism, in theological and spiritual depth, and in finding new approaches to pastoral practice. Faced with the reality of the Latin American situation the bishops were led to state their position on social and political structures and ideologies. On many points they endorsed the spirituality, theology and liberating pastoral praxis of progressive communities and movements. Their preoccupation with the completeness and purity of doctrine and their resolve to preserve the continuity of the ecclesiastical structures did not lead to the complete breakdown of the dialogue between the episcopal college and the dynamic forces which prevailed at ground level.

Many theological and pastoral insights, matured in practical life, were officially approved in spite of the tensions and conflicts which they aroused in Church and society.

Topics such as the theology of poverty, the importance of basic communities in the Church for the growth of conscientisation, integral liberation linked with the renewal of the Church, the closer adaptation of pastoral work to the 'people', appreciation of the prophetic witness, and many others are now definitely identified with the image of the official Latin American Church. They are bound to influence the Church as a whole, at least in the long run.

The debate on these topics was bound to expose the tensions and divisions within the Latin American Church and did not wholly overcome them. And yet, the Puebla document reveals the collective intent that the Church as such should contribute to the total liberation of Latin America.

Some points in this message to the Church as a whole need some brief clarification.

### 3. HOW CAN THE CHURCH BE WITH THE OPPRESSED PEOPLE OF LATIN AMERICA?

One of the key problems Puebla had to face was how the Church could genuinely and credibly proclaim God and Jesus Christ and be the living symbol of an integral liberation based on the gospel in a society which only too often and even in its basic structures denies and tramples on a human person's basic right to exist with dignity? How can a Church be a saving community and proclaim and demonstrate the 'Good News' in a society which calls itself officially 'Christian' but where the well-to-do minority sacrifices the vast majority to their own economic and social well-being, their political power and to the ideologies and false values which they impose on the majority through the mass media which they control?

In dealing with this, Puebla resisted the pressures of the economic, political and ideological forces which wanted to confine the Church to a purely religious and socially stabilising role, and expected the Church to capitulate blindly to the ideological manipulation not only of the gospel but of the Church's moral authority and its social influence.

What did Puebla do? It developed a project for evangelisation which integrated and gave a central position to a critically alert social *diakonia*, but it would not allow this to compete with the need for a deepening, celebration and proclamation of the faith or to be an excuse for the rejection of loyalty to the Church as 'mystery' and as 'institution'.

According to Puebla neither the future of authentic Christianity nor the liberation of the people gains anything from the Church's loss of identity or from the atomisation of God's people into small and radical groups. It is convinced that the Word of God is socially effective to the degree it is accepted in its original purity, is celebrated as such in community and confessed personally, and in so far as it is translated into ethically responsible and meaningfully viable projects without creating hysterical internal quarrels.

Secondary and even essential sections of this vision of the Church are open to revision. Here one thinks of Puebla's unrealistic appeal to a social teaching of the Church which is assumed to be free from any ideology and its reluctance to accept the progress made by the social sciences and to use the results to correct its own bland ethical and pastoral statements.

Yet, the overall trend of Puebla's conclusions is clear: faith in God must be free of any ideological misconceptions, and our words, our style of life and our commitment must bear witness to the truth that God can be recognised wherever men show integrity, liberate themselves and unite to resist historical situations which are rooted in oppression and injustice. The reason is that injustice is a form of idolatry and that God himself assumes the defence of the poor. It is at this point that theology begins to identify with the oppressed people of Latin America.

Puebla also shows a basic belief in the cultural values of the people, the genuine Christian character of its religious convictions and their expression of them as well as the historical power of the people's determination to achieve liberation. In spite of the present cultural crisis Puebla remains convinced that the true Latin American cultural identity resides in the people at large, rather than in the élite, and that this culture embodies the Christian (Catholic) soul of Latin America.

This position has far-reaching pastoral consequences. It means that Puebla judges that evangelisation is primarily addressed to the people as such, and that the people are consequently the primary partner and associate of the Church's evangelising activities. It calls on the élite to persevere in the dialogue with the people, to take part in the religious celebrations of and for the simple people, and to take its rôle as leaders and educators of the people seriously.

Even in the laborious and tense discussions about the ecclesial basic communities the cause of solidarity with the people won the day. Puebla encourages the growth of these communities because, among other things, it provides the ordinary people with a framework in which they can express, strengthen and purify their faith, build up a sense of responsibility with regard to the mission of the Church, and can become articulate, critically aware and committed citizens.

The consequences of this attitude of the bishops towards the religious character of the 'people' was that the challenge and legitimate questions put by a secular society to the faith and the Church only received apologetic and even superficial treatment. Over against this less than convincing approach there was, however, a determined effort to use key words which expressed the people's deeper awareness of values and their expectation, such as 'people on the way', 'community', 'integral liberation' and 'new society', and integrated them into their theology. It is likely that in Latin America in the future the Church will become a Church with and of the people as this impetus will gain in strength.

## 4. TOWARDS A PROPHETIC CHRISTIANITY

The final conclusions contain some remarkable statements by the bishops on social matters. Again and again they raise their voice against shocking social situations and practices and against the glaring social inequalities revealed in widespread extreme misery, exploitation, oppression and frustration. They clearly want to be recognised as the spokesmen for the oppressed.

Their analysis of the causes of oppression and underdevelopment comes closer than was expected to that of social scientists who attribute the problems of the Third World to its dependency on the affluent society and 'the unjust, offensive supremacy and domination of some peoples and social strata over other peoples and social strata'.[5]

They also defend the interests of the Third World against the expansionist policies of the First and the Second World when they demand that the cultural heritage of Latin America should be respected, and particularly when they accuse the economic, political and ideological power groups of having created this social chaos. Puebla's criticism of the dominant ideologies also shows that many bishops throughout the world not only condemn the fascism of the 'Doctrine of National Security' and Marxist collectivism but, starting from the peripheral situation of Latin America, they arrive at a radical criticism of the western capitalist system and its values in general. Thus this concentration on the 'dependency' situation constitutes a breakthrough in pastoral thinking about society and gives Puebla's concept of social sin a challenging and militant character.

The Church itself is prophetic only in so far as it is committed to the Word and witness of Him who identified with the victims of history, and therefore in so far as it, too, tries to identify with the marginalised and oppressed in their actual situation. This means that the Church must concentrate on rejecting the idol of power and money, developing a life-style of poverty to be one with the 'people' and 'gradually dissociating itself from those who hold economic or political power',[6] whatever sacrifices and conflicts this may imply.

The emergence of these dominant trends in its theological and pastoral preoccupations show that Puebla was feeling its way towards a qualitatively new way of living the faith and a new view of the Church.

*Translated by T. L. Westow*

## Notes

1. See Vincent Cosmao 'Le Tournant de Puebla' in *Foi et Développement* (1979) 65-67; 'A Distance de Puebla' in *Lumen Vitae* 3 (1979) 245-254; Norbert Greinacher *Kirche der Armen* (Munich 1980) 79-150; *Kontinent der Hoffnung*. Beiträge und Berichte zu Puebla edd. Hans Schöpfer and Emil Stehle (Munich/Mainz 1979); Hans Schöpfer *Lateinamerikanische Befreiungstheologie* (Stuttgart 1979) ch. 6; Michel Schooyans 'La Conférence de Puebla, un Risque, un Espoir' in *Nouvelle Revue Théologique* 5 (1979) 641-675.

2. Vincent Cosmao in the articles cited in note 1.

3. Juan Carlos Scannone 'Diverses interprétations latino-américaines du document de Puebla' in *Lumen Vitae* 2 (1980) 211-227.

4. *Puebla. Evangelisation at present and in the future of Latin America*. Conclusions (London, CIIR, 1980) nn. 368, 363, 647, 655.

5. *Ibid.*, n. 427.

6. *Ibid.*, nn. 623 and 144.

Paulo Evaristo Arns

# The Communion of the Churches in Society

INTRODUCTION

VATICAN II marked an advance in ecclesiology. The axis of thought was no longer *potestas*, but *communio*. The Church is communion in its essence and in its mission[1] and this is brought about both in its universal reality and in the particularity of local churches. In fact, this focus led to an exposition of the identity and originality of the local church[2] and of its relationship to the universal Church.[3]

As the local churches are embodied in the specificity of a particular culture, and give their evangelical witness within a specific, limited social structure, there is also a need for specific reflection on both the sociological meaning of unity and the achievement of universal communion. How can the universality of the Church become a sociological reality?

More specifically, the problem shows itself as a challenge at the very heart of the social process: how to live the unity and communion of the churches historically and sociologically in a divided world, and how to witness to communion in a society marked by structural conflict,[4] characterised and sustained by the consciousness, practice and organisation of different social groupings.

Reflection on the building of communion in the social fabric from this standpoint tries to show what form unity must take in a church living and witnessing to charity in a realistic and committed manner designed to contribute to the building of a juster and more equal society. It must do this not only in an idealistic 'formality', but in the effective bringing-about of a communion and common good in which all can effectively share, both in the relationship of the local churches among themselves and in their relationship to the universal Church, and in a specific witness embodied in a pluralist society.

## 1. THE UNITY OF THE CHURCH IN SOCIAL LIFE

This is not the place for a study of the overall mystery of the unity of the Church.[5] My subject rather comes under the heading of that unity which arises as a task or mission in a specific social context. On the unity of the Church, it is sufficient to refer to St Thomas' guidelines on unity and schism,[6] or Cajetan's famous commentary on the subject.

In effect, charity is the divine friendship uniting all members of the divine *koinonia*[7] to God and to one another. For mankind, in the specific historical state of humanity, this *communio* is the reunion of those redeemed by Christ Jesus the Redeemer of Mankind, through sharing in his grace. These make up the Body of Christ, the Church, a communion whose members are held together by the bond of charity, a sacramental and ordained charity, received from Christ through the sacraments and ordained, orientated by him, through the teaching he left as Prophet, Priest and King, to the fullness of life in the kingdom of God. Once communicated and ordained, this charity produces the unity of the Church, a communion of the faithful among themselves and under the One Head, Christ and his vicar on earth. It is this unity that constitutes the peace of the Church, the peace of Christ, which he gave us in the Spirit sent through the paschal mystery.[8]

Now, the division of societies and cultures, marked by the injustice present at the roots of the social process and the relationship between groups which make up the social fabric, force one to think more directly about how unity can be built up and experienced, in an effective manner and not only on a 'formal' plane hovering above specific historical and social divisions. The Church is not the world; it is the reality of the New Man as a sign for the world to believe and free itself from sin.[9] But, can the Church live a unity focused only on itself, in a world dominated by the sin of division and of domination through violence, injustice, segregation and marginalisation? How can the communion of love lived in the churches become meaningful and operative, and therefore sacramental?

## 2. LEVELS OF UNITY AND COMMUNION

In order to reach a more precise understanding of the question, it should be said that the Church does not appear to be universal in sociological terms. So what needs to be done in order to turn the universality of the Church into sociological fact? We need to define levels of ecclesial unity precisely.

### (a) Unity and visible communion

The unity of the Church in history was built on a dynamic *relationship*, in which each part, in its singular originality, united itself to the universal whole of the union of churches. Yet we need to decide on what level this unity of communion is brought about.

(i) There is first the unity of theologal life and the sacraments. All love, hope and believe in the same reality. They all receive the same sacraments. And yet, *if this were the only unity*, we could not say that the Church was one. We could only say that the faithful were like one another in these aspects.

(ii) Another aspect of ecclesial life consists in having the same head: Christ, or his vicar on earth. This constitutes a unity of order in relation to a principle; and also a union of action in the acts of ordaining and obeying. And yet here too, if Christian unity were no more than this, we could not say that the Church was one. The statement that we possess one head can also be applied to a federation of States whose only link is a central government but who also each retain their autonomy as political entities. The unity of the Church is not like that of a confederacy under a single head. It goes deeper than that.

(iii) We reach a deeper level when we see the communion of the faithful among themselves depending on the fact that they form *part of a community of which they are members*. This is a *relationship* of the parts to the whole, neither of which can exist without the other. It is a relationship of belonging to a totality. This requires action, and interaction, because each part depends on the whole and vice-versa.

F

The Spirit inspires each of the faithful, and each part of the Church, in its totality—universal or particular—to believe, hope and love, not only in accordance with the requirements of their particular acts, *but in union and accordance with what they should be as a whole*, as the reality of a member of the Body of the Church,[10] in a movement which sweeps beyond the mere parts and binds each to the whole, making each participate in the whole both in what it achieves and in what it receives.

Such a situation depends on the action of the Holy Spirit. It does not come about simply as a consequence of the existence of a collection of local churches. It is the life of the one Body in which each part acts on behalf of the whole, and in which the whole is present in each part. In this respect, ecclesiology needs to enrich itself with the patristic theology of trinitarian life: the unity and communion of the Churches, in its particularity and in its universal totality, besides being understood in the light of the Unity and Truth of the Body of Christ, should also be grasped in the perspective of the *perichoresis* of the life of the Trinity, in the strength of the Spirit who proceeds from the Father and the Son and unites them in one sole life of love in the originality of each divine person.[11] A patristic pneumatology could greatly enrich ecclesiology, which has long been captive in a uniform framework. So, unity of communion is the greater good in the order of individual relationships and in that of relationships between social groups: 'Cujus unitas est summum bonum, *non simpliciter sed in genere bonorum ad proximum spectantium*: utpote bonum totius mundi, non qualemcumque sed sprituale; non per accidens sed per se; non secundarim sed principale; qiua est *ipsum esse Ecclesiae ut unius totius* rationem habet.'[12]

It is this type of unity that leads us to understand the historical task of building and experiencing the ecclesial community through its presence and witness in a divided and conflictive society. Individuals, groups and classes can be united through love. The unity of the Church in the Spirit can only come from an effective and liberating love, which is charity lived on a political level and in a political dimension: 'Movet enim Spiritus Sanctus per caritatem singulos fideles ad volendum se esse partes unius collectionis catholicae, quam ipse vivificat; ac per hoc ad constituendam unam Ecclesiam catholicam.'[13]

## 2. BUILDING THE UNIVERSAL UNITY OF COMMUNION

Today, unity of communion depends on the *preferential option for the poor*. The universality of evangelical love is mediated through the particularity of disadvantaged social groups, from whom comes the call to build a *truly* just and fraternal universal brotherhood. This is the same as saying that the universality of communion of the Church in the unity of the love of Christ is mediated through the specific incarnation of love in the specificity of the individual local churches.

On the one hand, the universality of love is mediated through the particularity of preferential love: in the first place, this reveals the sin of division and injustice; in the second, it shows the way to a communitary and social life in which charity is no mere 'formality' (either on the idealistic level of what ought to be, or on that of unfulfilled intentions), empty and lacking a reality embracing both the parts and the whole of social structure, at all levels—economic, social, political and cultural. On the other hand, the option for the poor proclaims the love and justice of the kingdom-in-the-making through the Church, and through the local churches in specific social situations, the *effective* sign and seed of a new world. The preferential option for the poor is a stance adopted in favour of oppressed classes and races and the specific movement of charity in the Spirit aimed at building a universal communion going beyond mere formal expression, becoming a socio-historical reality. This reality comes up against the dynamic fact of the organisation of society into classes. Faced with this dynamic fact, the task of communion becomes one of constant criticism in the light of the gospel message, of the consciousness, practice and organisation of social groups according to their own interests and ideologies. Charity lived on the social level should go beyond simple relationships between individuals, into the dynamic of the relationship of the whole in itself, and of the parts with the whole. This relationship obeys a special dynamic that cannot be ignored in building unity and communion, if the ecclesial communion is truly to become a sign and instrument of the kingdom of God in a particular social structure;[14] the mystery of communion happens in the visible reality of history.[15]

This tension between the particular and the universal, between the part and the whole, points first to the need for communion within a local church—which must be the *adequate expression* in specific form of invisible communion, in the visible communion of one section of the people of God[16]—inserted into the social structure and specific cultural reality of a race or ethnic group, with its particular problems of domination and division of the means of production, division of labour, political power and cultural expressions.

This section of the people of God entrusted to a bishop builds its reality of communion by giving the specific witness of charity, bringing about unity (the relationship of the parts to the whole) within its ecclesial reality and within the social structure in which it is embodied, making charity in the Spirit transform all levels of this social reality. If it fails to do all this, the salvation of which this Church is a sign is 'reduced' in one of its aspects, and therefore shorn of its totality, and runs the risk of becoming an empty sign hovering over a reality in which salvation cannot take root, and in which the sin of division, injustice and domination will therefore predominate.

This same tension also explains the need for communion between local churches of a region of the world. The challenges of injustice and marginalisation should bring these churches to unite in charity among themselves, in the service of the solidarity that they should exercise in the context in which they organise themselves and give witness. In their quest for the common good, and for social conditions which overcome dominations and divisions, the churches are cementing and achieving effective unity of communion, in a socially and historically conditioned manner.

### 3. UNIVERSAL UNITY AND COMMUNION

Unity in love precedes and lays a basis for communion. It is its condition and the inner source of its truth and effective uniting dynamism. Love as '*vis unitiva et concretiva*', in the sense given it by pseudo-dionysius, is certainly the most specific and fruitful way of understanding both the originality of the parts and the cohesion of the whole, in the life of the local churches and the communion of the universal Church.

In this scheme, unity does not in fact mean uniformity. Just as the Father and the Son, in the mutual gift of the Spirit, are united in one life while keeping the irreducible originality of two persons, so communication between the churches should be based on this same dynamism. Necessary local options should be respected, as should the organisations necessary to enable the churches to give their witness of charity and life.

The relationship of the churches among themselves, and with the universal unity of the Church, or the relationship between the churches of the periphery (Third World) and those of the centre (churches of the First World and particularly the Roman Church), thus becomes a dynamic reality and a '*vis concretiva*' proper to the love and inspiration of the Spirit; it is a reality of relationship, and therefore dynamic and active, ordered to the good of mankind, since in its innermost reality the Church is a sacrament of *salvation*.

This is the source of the communion and cooperation of the churches, so necessary today if they are to carry out their work of evangelisation. Thanks to this communion, every church has a care for all the others, and shares its needs with all. They all communicate their concerns to each other, since the building up of the Body of Christ is the duty of the whole episcopal college, and of all the local churches, in their reality as sections of the people of God embodied in specific social situations and cultures.

The successor of Peter, for his part, is the visible head of this unity of communion. And as it is made up of many members, the episcopal college expresses the variety and universality of the people of God; while as it is united under a sole head, it expresses and brings out the unity of the flock of Christ, which is a gift of the Spirit. In it, the bishops, faithfully respecting the primacy of their head, enjoy their own powers[17] for the good of their faithful, and even for the good of the whole Church, always with the help of the Holy Spirit, the organic structure and source of harmony in the Church.[18]

The tension between the particularity of each local church and the universal communion as a sociological fact requires more specific comment. Much has in fact been said and written about the position of the bishops in our countries and about the attitude of the pope to them. Yet the documents of the Brazilian Bishops' Conference continually demonstrate that there is a basic unity within a variety of situations and temperaments. This was shown when the national episcopate put forward its 'Christian Requirements for a Political Order'. There have never been great differences in the analysis of the socio-economic aspects of the country. The great majority of the bishops, priests and people are in constant contact with the poverty, sufferings and differing forms of exploitation of the people. The great problem was that of the rural areas, and it was the exodus from these that produced the over-rapid urbanisation and consequent growth of the shanty-towns around the great cities. The bishops have been pronouncing on the problem since 1950, and set out their position in a memorable document published in that year, from which only four out of 200 dissented. The words addressed by Pope John-Paul II to the national conference during his recent visit confirm the importance of this unity and this communion of the churches, in their singularity, with the head of the episcopal college.

The pope's words to the workers, in the Morumbi Stadium in São Paulo, also encourages us to re-state that the reality of communion takes on substance—since love is a 'vis concretiva'—through a historical project of which the Church is witness and messenger. This project is a complex one; to bring about the kingdom and civilisation of love, as the pope said, is a difficult, complex task which has to be renewed and perfected according to the particular needs of social situations.

The unity of the Church's witness does not come about through a monolithic body of formulas for action in society, but from the originality of approach by each church in fidelity to the basic quest for the kingdom in answer to the calls of the oppressed classes and downtrodden races. Pope Paul VI had in fact already said that the social teaching of the Church was not a monolithic whole, but had to be embodied in an ever-new dynamism according to the particular features of each situation.[19] Its embodiment according to the needs of different places and times will always be the result of discernment in intelligent and courageous love for the greater truth and efficacy of the good news of salvation.

Furthermore, the historical project is mediated through the democratic reality of pluralist societies. Here the churches are servants, supporting modes that most favour the real communion of the whole people, in which most can share and benefit from the goods of civilisation, human values and those of the kingdom of God. The building of communion is the service the Church gives to society, alongside and in union with those who strive for a new social order.[20] Meanwhile, the experience of communion at different levels of the local church and in all the local churches that make up a country, a continent or the whole of Catholicism, provides a vital service in social cohesion and transformation. This is perhaps the essential answer to the question of how the universality of the Church can become a sociological fact. The dynamism of *participation and communion* proposed by Puebla could be turned into a programme, not only for the local churches, but also for a project of evangelisation for the whole of the Third World, and for the relationship between this and the churches of the First World. There is an increasing and widespread need for centres of participation and communion capable of changing the whole texture of the social and cultural fabric. If this dynamism could become an effective and normative reality in the structure of the churches and of their mission, in relations between the local churches and their relationship to the unity of the universal Church, then communion would certainly become a sociological reality, and the full unity of the Church would increasingly become that sign which Jesus Christ wished his followers to be in the world.[21]

*Translated by Paul Burns*

## Notes

1. LG § 1h.
2. CD § 11.
3. EN § 62.
4. Puebla, 1209.
5. See Y. Congar *L'Eglise, une sainte, catholique et apostolique, Myst. Sal.* 15 (Paris 1970).
6. ST 2a-2ae. Q. 39 and Cardinal Cajeton's Commentary thereto.
7. 1 John 1:1-4.
8. See John 20:21.
9. See John 17.
10. See 1 Cor. 12.
11. See Sts Ignatius of Antioch, Irenaeus, Basil, etc.
12. Cardinal Cajetan's Commentary to 2a-2ae. Q. 39, art. 1.
13. *Ibid.*
14. See LG §§ 1 and 5.
15. LG § 8.
16. LG § 8; CD § 11.
17. CD § 8.
18. See LG § 22.
19. See *Octogesima Adveniens* § 4.
20. See Puebla, Pt. 4.
21. John 17.

# PART IV

*Bulletin*

Final Document

# International Ecumenical Congress of Theology
# 20 February-2 March 1980, São Paulo, Brazil

INTRODUCTION

1. WE, CHRISTIANS from forty-two countries, meeting in the city of São Paulo from 20 February to 2 March 1980, held the Fourth International Ecumenical Congress of Theology, convened by the Ecumenical Association of Third World Theologians.

At the same time we have shared our reflections with the Christian communities who have been meeting at the Theology Week each night at the Catholic University in São Paulo.

One hundred and eighty persons of various Christian churches including laity, bishops, pastors, priests, religious, and theologians, participated in the Congress. We came from the popular[1] Christian communities spread throughout Latin America and the Caribbean; we have also come from Africa and Asia and from the ethnic minorities of the United States; observers from Europe and North America were also present.

The Congresses of Dar-es-Salaam (Tanzania) in 1976, Accra (Ghana) in 1977, and Colombo (Sri Lanka) in 1979 preceded this Fourth Congress.

2. The theme of our meeting was 'Ecclesiology of the Popular Christian Communities'. Our reflection took as its starting point the rich experience of these basic ecclesial communities, sign of the renewal of the churches of the Third World, and was concentrated particularly on Latin America. In this experience we find ourselves profoundly linked to our churches and pastors, faithful to the appeal of the Word of God as well as to the involvement of the Christian communities in the life of our peoples.

3. Catholics and Protestants from various churches, we admit to a common search in the establishment of the kingdom of justice and peace. In reflecting on the practice of the popular Christian communities, we shared days of community prayer, praising the Lord for all the signs of liberation and pleading on behalf of those who still suffer the destitution of captivity.

4. Challenged by the Word of God, which comes to us through the Bible and the history of our peoples, and as members of the community of Jesus Christ, we now give witness to the results of our work.

5. But first we want to express our deep gratitude to Cardinal Paulo Evaristo Arns for the fraternal hospitality with which he received us in his archdiocese.

We also appreciate the messages of support received from Rev. Philip Potter, general secretary of the World Council of Churches, from Cardinal J. Willebrands, president of the Secretariat for Christian Unity, and from Bishop Frederico Pagura, president of the Latin American Council of Churches.

## 1. THE IRRUPTION OF THE POOR INTO HISTORY

### (a) Popular Liberation Movements

6. The situation of suffering, misery, and exploitation of the great majority of human beings, concentrated especially but not exclusively in the so-called Third World, is as undeniable as it is unjust.

7. Nevertheless, the most important historical process of our times has begun to be led by these very people, the truly 'wretched of the earth'. Their oppression finds its roots in the colonial system of exploitation of which they were victims for centuries. Their struggle to defend their lives, to preserve their racial and cultural identity, denied by the foreign oppressor, is as widespread as this domination. But it is clear that their determination and their capacity for human liberation have today an outreach never before equalled, as we see in the recent case of Nicaragua.

8. In the context of the Third World, the emerging popular classes generate social movements; in their struggles is forged a more lucid consciousness of society as a whole as well as of themselves.

9. These popular social movements express much more than an economic grievance. They represent a phenomenon, new in our times: the massive irruption of the poor in every society. These are the exploited classes, the oppressed races, people who some would hope to keep anonymous or absent from human history, and who, with increasing determination, show their own faces, proclaim their word, and organise to win by their own efforts the power that will permit them to guarantee the satisfaction of their needs and the creation of authentic conditions of liberation.

10. In the case of Latin America, alongside the industrial workers' movement, whose strength has traditionally been recognised, and the peasants' union organisation, which includes vast masses of the impoverished, new forms of workers' organisations are arising, broader opposition groups within the unions, as well as popular social movements originating at the local level, e.g., neighbourhood associations, mothers' clubs, movements against the high cost of living, for better housing, for better health conditions, etc. From the deepest levels of our poor, the oppressed indigenous nations affirm their ancient identity and oppressed races fight to shake off their ethnic oppression within the popular movement as a whole. It is a complex and discontinuous process, with advances and setbacks; nevertheless, it shows an ever-ascending tendency that is a sign of hope.

11. To the degree that the popular movement develops, the fundamental question of formulating a broad historical project is posed. Today such a historical project is based on the critique of capitalism and of imperialist domination. It includes a radical demand for democratisation in the construction of a political system in which popular control over those who govern as well as popular power are effective realities.

### (b) Structures of Domination

12. This historical journey of the people of the Third World takes place within the

framework of dependent capitalism. In that system the sectors that hold economic, political, and cultural power exercise their domination over society by means of an enormous number of structures, institutions, and mechanisms, which are multiplied at the national and international levels, and which vary according to each country and region: unequal ownership of the land, concentration of wealth and of technico-scientific discoveries, the armament race with its production of weapons and destruction of life, transnationalisation of the economy, etc. At the international level this is effected by means of monetary mechanisms, multinational corporations, political decision-making clubs for the rich nations (e.g., the Trilateral Commission), leading the nations of the Third World into an ever increasing foreign debt.

13. In the African, Asian, and Latin American societies, with specific characteristics in each region, the international structures in conjunction with the national structures of the capitalist system produce a process of development which is concentrated for the benefit of the few, with the consequent impoverishment of the masses, increase in the cost of living, inflation, unemployment, undernourishment, deterioration of the quality of life, super-exploitation of women and children, etc.

14. The dominant sectors exercise their power in society by means of the internalisation of certain attitudes and behaviour through formal education, the mass media, political parties, and even popular organisations. Thus, a certain type of society is being shaped with its materialistic and utilitarian values and life-styles.

15. Furthermore, power is concentrated in authoritarian States which, from the top down, consider themselves as the protectors of society, penetrating even the private lives of the citizens. This procedure is justified in Latin America by models of restricted democracy, which are such only in form, or of national security.

The political institutions, at every level, restrict and try to control the participation of the popular groups and classes in making decisions and in effecting social change.

16. It is also important to stress the implacability of a whole series of mechanisms of a more subtle domination, often underestimated in the analyses, which produce forms of inequality and discrimination among blacks, indigenous peoples, and women. It has to be noted that the different mechanisms are not opposed, nor even juxtaposed, one to the other, but on the contrary, are articulated in one and the same comprehensive structure of domination. The black populations, the indigenous peoples, and the women of the popular classes have been for centuries, and are still today, doubly oppressed; more than in the past, however, they are struggling for their liberation. These mechanisms respond neither in a deterministic nor a linear manner to the interests of domination, but rather give rise to contradictions that the popular sectors can use to their own benefit on their journey.

17. In reality, these structures and mechanisms of domination follow different rhythms according to the different nations and regions, especially according to the varied capacity for response—in terms of organisation, awareness, and struggle—of the popular social forces that are emerging. Thus, these forces are constantly occupying more space in the various institutions of society.

18. Furthermore, it is clear that this system of domination has been in a permanent state of crisis from the very beginning, even though this crisis has become increasingly more acute in the last few decades with the strengthening of the popular sectors.

### (c) Popular Movement and Basic Ecclesial Communities

19. Today in Latin America there is at the heart of the popular movement a growing number of Christians who explicitly express and celebrate their faith in Christ and their hope in the kingdom of God. A popular, ecclesial stream is emerging that expresses itself in various forms of Christian life and community.

20. The irruption of the poor also is occurring within the established Church, producing a religious and ecclesial transformation. The Church is experiencing the judgment of God, which breaks into the liberating history of the poor and exploited. It is a moment of ecclesial grace and conversion, an inexhaustible source of a new and demanding spiritual experience. In the people's struggle, the Church continues to rediscover its own identity and mission.

21. This Christian stream within the popular movement and the renewal of the Church from the standpoint of its option for the poor constitute a unique and specific movement in the Church. This movement takes shape in different types of basic ecclesial communities, where the people find a space for resistance, struggle, and hope in the face of domination. There the poor celebrate their faith in the liberating Christ and discover the political dimension of love.

22. The basic ecclesial communities, or popular Christian communities, form an integral part of the people's march, but do not constitute a movement or political power parallel to the popular organisations, nor do they seek to legitimate them. The Christian communities—through consciousness-raising, popular education, and the development of ethical and cultural values—exercise among the poor a liberating ministry that is an integral part of their specific mission of evangelisation, prophecy, pastoral care, and ministering the sacraments.

23. The Church redeems the people's symbols of hope, manipulated for centuries by the system of domination. The Church celebrates the presence of the God of life in the people's struggles for a more just and human life. The Church encounters the God of the poor by confronting the idols of oppression. The Church receives the kingdom as a free gift of the Father in the building of brotherhood and the solidarity of all the oppressed classes and races, humiliated by this anti-kingdom of discrimination, violence, and death that is the dominant capitalist system.

24. The historical manifestation of the poor who appropriate the gospel as a source of inspiration and hope in their struggle for freedom is deeply rooted in the biblical tradition. It can, moreover, be easily verified over the course of the history of the Christian churches.

25. In the Old Testament the entire history of a people in the process of liberation is told from the standpoint of their exodus from a situation of oppression and towards a space and time of freedom, abundance, and brotherhood. The same occurs in the New Testament, where the teaching of Jesus, in Matthew, starts with the beatitudes of the poor (Matt. 5:2-11) and ends with the definitive affirmation that Christ can be encountered only in concrete actions that redeem the poor from their condition of exploitation, oppression, hunger, that is, of being stripped of their human dignity as children of God (Matt. 25:31-40).

26. The whole of the biblical record reveals that the struggles of the poor for their liberation are signs of God's action in history, and as such are experienced as imperfect and provisional seeds of the definitive kingdom. Christians are responsible for discerning the action of the Spirit, who moves history forward and who creates a foretaste of the kingdom in every part of the world of the poor.

## 2. CHALLENGE TO THE ECCLESIAL CONSCIENCE

27. This path of suffering, of a growing consciousness, and of the struggle of our people poses questions and challenges for us as Christians and as Church. On the one hand, we must understand this journey in the light of God's revelation throughout history. On the other hand, our ways of living and understanding the faith are challenged by the vitality and creativity of the popular movements and the basic

ecclesial communities. In a special way we need to bring up to date and deepen our ecclesiology, mainly along three lines: (*a*) the profound relationship between the kingdom, human history, and the Church; (*b*) evangelisation and the basic ecclesial communities; and (*c*) the following of Jesus.

### (*a*) Kingdom, Human History and Church

28. By our faith we know that the collective history that we live with our people, with its contradictions of domination and liberation, of segregation and fraternity, of life and death, has a sense of hope. Here we want 'to give the reason for our hope' (1 Pet. 3:15).

29. The God we believe in is the God of life, of liberty, and of justice. God created 'the world and all that is in it' for man and woman so that they might live, communicate life, and transform this world into a home for all their children. The sin of human beings, who take the earth unto themselves and murder their brother, does not destroy God's plan (Gen. 2-4). So God calls Abraham to be the father of a people (Gen. 12ff.) and Moses to free that people from oppression, to make a covenant with it, and to guide it to the promised land (Exod., Deut.).

30. Jesus proclaims the new presence of God's kingdom to this same people. The kingdom that Jesus points to with his messianic practice is the efficacious will of the Father who desires life for all his children (Luke 4, 7:18-23). The meaning of Jesus' existence is to give his life so that we all might have life, and abundantly. He did this in solidarity with the poor, becoming poor himself (2 Cor. 8:9; Phil. 2:7) and in that poverty announced the kingdom of liberation and life. The religious élite and political leaders that controlled Jesus' people rejected this gospel: they 'took from their midst' the Witness to the Father's love, and 'they killed the Author of life', Thus the 'sin of the world' reached its limit (Acts 2:23; 3:14-15; Rom. 1:18-32; John 1:5, 10-11; 3:17-19).

31. But God's love is greater than human sin. The Father carries his work forward, for the Jewish people and for all the peoples of the world, through Jesus' resurrection from the dead. In the risen Christ we have the definitive triumph over death and the first fruits of 'the new heaven and the new earth', the city of God among humankind (Rev. 21:1-4).

32. The kingdom does not have the same kind of tangible presence for us as it did for Jesus' companions (1 John 1), nor can we yet see the fullness of the kingdom we hope for. Therefore the risen Lord pours out his Spirit on the community of his disciples, so that by its very life the Church might be the visible body of Christ among human beings, revealing his liberating activity in history (Acts 2; 1 Cor. 11-12; Eph. 4).

33. The coming of the kingdom as God's final design for his creation is experienced in the historical process of human liberation.

On the one hand the kingdom has a Utopian character, for it can never be completely achieved in history; on the other hand, it is foreshadowed and given concrete expression in historical liberations. The kingdom pervades human liberations; it manifests itself *in* them, but it is not identical *with* them. Historical liberations, by the very fact that they are historical, are limited, but are open to something greater. The kingdom transcends them. Therefore it is the object of our hope and thus we can pray to the Father: 'Thy kingdom come'. Historical liberations incarnate the kingdom to the degree that they humanise life and generate social relationships of greater fraternity, participation, and justice.

34. To help us understand the relationship between the kingdom and historical liberations we might use the analogy of the mystery of the Incarnation. Just as in one and the same Jesus Christ the divine and the human presence each maintain their identities,

without being absorbed or confused, so too is the eschatological reality of the kingdom and historical liberations.

35. The liberation and life offered by God surpass everything that we can achieve in history. But these are not offered outside history nor by bypassing history. It is all too clear, however, that there are other forces in the world, those of oppression and death. These are the forces of sin, personal and social, that reject the kingdom and, in practice, deny God.

36. All people are called by the word of the gospel to receive the kingdom as a gift, to be converted from injustice and from idols to the living and true God, proclaimed by Jesus (Mark 1:15; John 16:3; 1 Thess. 1:9). The kingdom is grace and must be received as such, but it is also a challenge to new life, to commitment, to liberation and solidarity with the oppressed in the building of a just society. Thus we say that the kingdom is *of God*; it is grace and God's work. But at the same time it is a demand and a task for human beings.

37. The kingdom is the horizon and meaning of the Church. In the Third World context we must recall that the Church does not exist for itself, but to serve human beings in the building of the kingdom of God, revealing to them the power of the kingdom present in history, witnessing to the presence of Christ the Liberator and to his Spirit in the events and in the signs of life in the people's march.

In fulfilment of its mission the Church seeks to follow Jesus, taking its stand with him on behalf of the poor, 'pitching its tent' among them (John 1:14). Thus it can live in an intense and meaningful way the new reality of the kingdom. From this starting point it can be a credible witness and living sacrament of the Good News of the kingdom for all human beings.

38. The kingdom also judges the Church. It incites it to conversion, denouncing its contradictions, its personal and structural sins. It makes it confess its historical mistakes, its complicities, and the betrayal of its evangelising mission. And in this act of humble confession the Church encounters the grace of the Lord that purifies it and encourages it on its pilgrimage.

### (b) Evangelisation and the Basic Ecclesial Communities

39. A community is Christian because it evangelises: this is its task, its reason for being, its life. Evangelising is a diverse and complex activity. A Christian community is called to evangelise in all that it does, by word and by works.

40. To evangelise is to announce the true God, the God revealed in Christ, the God who makes a covenant with the oppressed and defends their cause, the God who liberates his people from injustice, from oppression, and from sin.

41. The liberation of the poor is a journey full of grief, marked by both the passion of Christ and by the signs of resurrection. The liberation of the poor is a vast history that embraces all of human history and gives it true meaning. The gospel proclaims the history of total liberation as it is present in today's events. It shows how, here and now, among the poor masses of Latin America and all marginated peoples, God is freeing his people.

42. Puebla spoke of 'the evangelising potential of the poor' (no. 1147). With this expression, Puebla wanted to recognise the rich and varied experience of many Christian communities. For it was this lived experience that allowed for the rediscovery of an evangelisation carried out by the poor. The poor—a believing, oppressed people—announce and demonstrate the presence of God's kingdom in their own journey, in their struggle: new life, the resurrection manifested in their communities, is living testimony that God is acting in them. Their love of their brothers and sisters, their love of their enemies, and their solidarity, show forth the active presence of the Father's

love. The poor can evangelise because the secrets of God's kingdom have been revealed to them (Matt. 11:25-27).

43. In Latin America evangelisation carried out by the poor has its privileged locus in a concrete experience: the basic ecclesial communities. In these communities is incarnated a Church that is, by vocation, continuously born of the people's faith, of 'those not invited to the banquet' (Luke 14:15-24). In them a committed life of faith is subjected to evaluation. In them the hope of the poor is celebrated and bread is shared, the bread that so many lack and in which the life of the Risen One is present and acknowledged. They are privileged places in which the people read the Bible and in their own words and with their own expressions make its message their own. These communities allow for moments of fraternal encounter in which God is recognised as Father. The community dimension is joined with the evangelising task, with the call to make disciples and to form an assembly of disciples, a Church of the poor.

44. The purpose of evangelisation is not the formation of small élite or privileged groups in the Church. It is addressed to the flock without a shepherd, as Jesus says (Matt. 9:35), that is, to the abandoned masses, dispossessed of all their goods. Therefore, the Christian communities are renewed in the movement that leads them to seek out the most exploited of the poor. Evangelisation of the masses is carried out within the perspective of the preferential option for the poor.

45. It thus contributes significantly to transforming the masses into a people. On the other hand, human multitudes are not isolated individuals. The poor are downtrodden together, with regard to what brings them together and gives them their identity: their culture, their language, their race, their nationality, and their history; this is doubly true in the case of women.

Evangelisation is a concrete activity that is addressed to concrete people, here and now. Thus it undertakes the liberation of the poor through the liberation of their culture, their language, their race, and their sex. The popular Christian communities are the first fruits of the whole people at whose service they are. In them the poor people better discover their identity, their worth, their evangelising mission within the history of the liberation of the poor. The universality of the gospel proclamation passes through this historical process and through this commitment of the Christian community.

### (c) Following Christ

46. The crowds who follow Jesus and are amazed at the good he does for all (Acts 10:38) are the first to hear the Good News of the kingdom. Jesus 'gathers around him a few human beings chosen from various social and political strata of the day. Though confused and often unfaithful, they are moved by the love and the power that radiates from him. They are the ones who constituted the foundation of his church. Drawn by the Father, they start out on the path involving the following of Jesus (Puebla, no. 192).

The power of the Spirit leads to conversion, to a radical change of life; thus an apostolic community is constituted, the seed and the model of the first ecclesial communities. In God's plan, if the rich and powerful of this world are to receive the gospel, they must learn it from the people.

47. These first communities witnessed to Jesus Christ and taught the way to follow him: Jesus was poor and lived among the poor and proclaimed hope to them. This was a messianic hope, different from certain erroneous notions of his time, but a faithful fulfilment of the Father's promise. The Messiah announces God's kingdom, that is, a God who is revealed as such because he reigns by doing justice to the poor and oppressed. To separate God from his kingdom is to not know the God proclaimed by Jesus, a God who calls together brothers and sisters from among the poorest and most abandoned. Jesus proclaims that they are blessed and that the kingdom belongs to them

as a gratuitous and preferential gift of the Lord. This gift brings with it the demand of a commitment to justice.

48. The Good News that announces to the poor the end of oppression, of deceit, of hypocrisy, and of the abuse of power, is also bad news for those who profit from this abuse and injustice. Thus the powerful persecute Jesus unto death. Jesus 'chose to be the decisive victim of the world's injustice and evil' (Puebla, no. 194) and so practise what he had taught: that none have greater love than those who give their lives for others. By such great love we will be recognised as his disciples. Such are 'the demands of the justice of God's kingdom in a radical and obedient discipleship' (letter to the Christian churches and Ecumenical Organisations of Latin America, Oaxtepec, Mexico, 24 September 1978).

49. The first communities walked the liberating path of Jesus Christ, proclaiming him as the one Lord. They were martyred for rejecting the idolatrous worship of the powerful of this world. Today many popular Christian communities in the Third World walk the same path in following Jesus. They refuse to accept the mechanisms of domination that enrich the powerful sectors and countries with the poverty of the weak (see the Address of Pope John-Paul II to the Episcopal Conference at Puebla). For the oppressed and exploited they claim justice and dignity, work and bread, education, shelter, and participation in the building of each people's history. In this liberating struggle these communities experience the Lord as alive and present. They feel the action of the Spirit who both calls them to trial in the desert and sends them to evangelise the poor and the oppressed with the courage of a new Pentecost.

50. In the following of Jesus the spiritual experience is never separated from the liberating struggle. In the heart of this process God is experienced as a Father to whom every effort and every struggle is offered. From him come bravery and courage, truth and justice. Filial trust assures that if the Father raised his Son to demonstrate the truth of his Word, he will also give life to those who, in the path of Jesus, give their lives for others.

51. Those who denounce destitution and oppression have, like Jesus, been persecuted. This denunciation unmasks the illusion of continuous, unlimited progress. Moreover it proclaims that the poor demand justice. These are uncomfortable truths that must not be silenced.

52. Jesus' journey, that of the basic ecclesial communities, is a journey of faith in a God whom we do not see and of a love of our brothers and sisters whom we do see. Those who say they believe, but do not love, or who say that they love but in practice do not, are not on Jesus' path. Thus the martyrs of justice, who give their lives for the freedom of their oppressed brothers and sisters, are also martyrs of faith, for they learn from the gospel the commandment of fraternal love as a sign of the Lord's disciples.

### 3. DEMANDS AND QUESTIONS

#### (a) Spirituality and Liberation

53. During our meeting we have dedicated a good deal of time to the common celebration of our faith and our hope.

54. We believe that cultivating spirituality, or life according to the Spirit of Jesus, is a fundamental demand placed on every one of us and on the Christian communities. Many of us, many of our communities, are living the search for Christian spirituality in the new conditions of the Church in the Third World.

Because of its crucial importance we think that the theme of spirituality must be taken up again in future meetings, writings, and events.

55. We must help our communities to appropriate the great spiritual tradition of the

Church that today, as in every age, is incarnated and expressed by taking up the present challenges of history. Thus, we can speak of a 'spirituality of liberation'. We must revitalise, and even at times recover, Christian spirituality as the original experience that drives Christians and the popular communities into an evangelising political commitment and theological reflection.

56.  This implies continually overcoming dualisms alien to biblical spirituality: faith and life, prayer and action, commitment and daily work, contemplation and struggle, creation and salvation. Spirituality is not merely a distinct moment in the process of the liberation of the poor. It is the mystique of the experience of God within this process. It means the encounter with the living God of Jesus Christ in collective history and in daily personal life. Prayer and commitment are not alternative practices; they require and mutually reinforce one another. Prayer is not an evasion but a fundamental way of following Jesus that makes us ever ready for the encounter with the Father and for the demands of our mission.

57.  Spirituality also demands of us today that we enrich ourselves with the great religious and cultural traditions of the Third World. All this will teach us to introduce poetry, music, symbols, festivity, fellowship, and above all the gratuitous dimension into the celebration of our faith.

58.  The agents of evangelisation are not to celebrate for the people but rather with them. The people evangelise us by passing on to us the mystique of their faith, their solidarity, and their struggles.

59.  The spirituality that we today seek to revitalise ought to emphasise the love of God that calls us to follow Jesus and is revealed in the poor. In the struggles, in the commitment, in the martyrdom of the people, Jesus is followed not only to the sacrifice of the cross, but also to his liberating resurrection.

60.  In the spirituality that we want to recreate, the option in solidarity with the poor and the oppressed becomes an experience of the God of Jesus Christ. All this demands a continual coming out of self and a change of social and cultural position. It commits us to live the political and economic consequences of the commandment of love.

61.  The Eucharist, or the Supper of the Lord, should hold the central place in our communities, together with the sharing of the Word of God. When they are celebrated among the poor and oppressed they are both promise and demand of justice, of the freedom and the fellowship for which the peoples of the Third World are struggling.

62.  For the Christian communities, Mary, the mother of Jesus, is seen above all as the poor, free, and committed woman of the Magnificat, as the faithful believer who accompanied her son to the Pasch. For the Catholic communities, the saints of their devotions become family in the kingdom and companions on the way.

63.  Our popular Christian communities should grow in their contemplative dimension. In their prayer, these communities of the Third World must be grateful for nature and life, because of the joy these produce in us. They should also be grateful for the gift of communion with the God who supports all in history. Besides living our prayer, our Christian communities must educate for it. Open to life, they will include in their prayer the cry of the people who demand justice and seek without rest the face of their liberating God.

64.  We believe, finally, in the liberating and evangelising efficacy of prayer—in ourselves and in the people. We believe in its humanising efficacy in the struggles. We believe that Christian contemplation gives sense to life and to history, even in the failures, and leads us to accept the cross as the way of liberation.

## (b) Persecution, Repression and Martyrdom

65.  The Church that is reborn by the power of the Spirit among the exploited and

G

oppressed classes of our peoples keeps alive the dangerous memory of the martyrs, who laid down their lives as a sign of their great love (John 15:13). With a genuinely Christian feeling this Church thus recovers the tradition of the most ancient Christian communities and touches the heart of Christian faith: the recovery from the hands of an impious, unjust, and idolatrous world of the maligned memory of one who was excluded from human society—Jesus of Nazareth.

66.  Besides putting an end to his life, the murder of Jesus (Acts 5:30) was intended to malign his reputation and deal a mortal blow to his cause: 'He has blasphemed' (Mark 14:64); 'if he were not a subversive we would not have brought him to this tribunal' (John 18:30); if they do not put a guard on his grave, 'his disciples will come and steal the body and tell the people that he rose from the dead' (Matt. 27:64).

67.  The dominant powers of Jesus' time were afraid that the one they had murdered would be remembered. However, the empty tomb and the power of the Spirit that made the risen Jesus present again among his friends stirred up the Easter faith that freed the disciples from a paralysing fear. Timid people proclaimed vigorously that this man 'killed outside the city wall' (Heb. 13:12), this Jesus whom you crucified, was raised by God and made Lord and Christ (Act 2:32, 36).

68.  The 'way of life', of 'way', that the disciples proclaimed, that common mind and heart, having all things in common and not allowing the exploitation of anyone, that 'effectiveness' in the proclamation of the risen Christ, in a word, that coming of the kingdom that the early Christian communities embodied (see Acts 4:32-35), was persecuted and repressed by the same people who murdered the Lord. United in the common life, in prayer and the breaking of the bread (Acts 2:42), those who before were silent through terror joined the resistance, full of the Spirit, and proclaimed that 'we have to obey God rather than men' (Acts 5:30).

69.  Throughout the Third World today the popular classes and oppressed ethnic minorities resist, organise, and struggle to build lands of cooperative, humanising justice, work and life. They are thus obeying God, who wills that people should live and dominate the earth as heirs, as children who feel that they are in a home of brothers and sisters. The Church, which is reborn of this people, in spontaneous and organised struggles, shares this struggle and often encourages it with its unshakeable faith in the love of God that guarantees the ultimate meaningfulness of this struggle.

70.  For this reason the Church suffers the same repression that the dominating classes visit on the people. This repression, unleashed out of hatred for justice, hatred for human dignity, is what today we call persecution of the Church. We have the right to celebrate as martyrs the tortured, the disappeared, the exiled, the imprisoned, and the murdered of this people. They are workers, peasants, indigenous peoples, and blacks, men and women and innocent children caught up in their parents' political commitment. They are also catechists, ministers of the Word, leaders of Christian communities, priests and pastors, men and women in religious orders, bishops and martyrs, whom we have the right to celebrate as heroes sacrificed from among the poor.

71.  When our Church does not consent to live a life generously surrendered for the cause of God in the cause of today's exploited and oppressed classes, when it allows itself to be paralysed with fear and does not remember its martyrs in solidarity with the people, we have the right to ask if it has new eyes to recognise the crucified Lord in the disfigured faces of the impoverished people of the Third World (see Puebla, nos. 31-39).

72.  We have the right to ask whether as a Church we live out the prayer of agony that Jesus lived out, the prayer of submission to the Father and of resistance to the oppressor, the prayer that gave Jesus the strength to follow the way of the cross, from which God raised him up. We have to ask our Church, if it recognises the 'greater love' in giving up one's life for one's friends.

73. Nevertheless, we give thanks to God because of the growing number of pastors and communities who proclaim the death of their martyrs and extend it with their own witness.

### (c) Unity of the Churches starting from the poor

74. The greatest division and disunity that the Third World suffers is the sin of injustice, through which 'the many have little and the few have much' (Puebla, Message to the Peoples of Latin America). This injustice goes beyond and also divides all our churches and leads them to take diverse and contradictory positions.

75. We affirm with joy that through solidarity with the cause of the poor, through participation in their just struggles, in their sufferings, and in their persecution, the first great barrier that for so long has divided our different churches is being broken down. Many Christians are rediscovering the gift of unity as they encounter the one Christ in the poor of the Third World (Matt. 25). The promotion of total liberation, the common suffering, and the sharing of the hopes and joys of the poor have put in clear relief all that we Christians hold in common.

76. In this option for the poor and in the practice of justice, we have deepened the roots of our faith in the one Lord, the one Church, the one God and Father. In the following of Jesus we confess Christ as the Son of God and the brother of all people. In the struggle for a just life for the poor we confess the one God, Father of all. In our ecclesial commitment we confess the Church of Jesus Christ as his body in history and as sacrament of liberation.

77. In this faith and practice the various popular Christian communities, Catholic and Protestant, share the same historical and eschatological vision. That faith and practice lead us forward in unity at the levels of evangelisation, liturgical celebration, doctrine and theology. If it is true that the poor evangelise us, it is also true that they open the way towards our unity. They accelerate the fulfilment of the last testament of Jesus, that all may be one, that all, Catholic and Protestant, and even more, all men and women of all races and cultures, may come to form the people of the children of God.

### (d) Churches and peoples of the Third World

78. In this Congress, with its profound encounters, we have noted a considerable lack of knowledge of one another and a lack of permanent, effective communion between our peoples and churches of Asia, Africa, America, the Caribbean and the ethnic minorities of the USA.

79. We cannot fail to recognise in each of the peoples and churches of the Third World their own identities and distinct contributions in the process of liberation: through the sufferings, struggles, and achievements of their respective histories and through the specific richness of their cultures. These are facets of the countenance of a poor, oppressed humanity that is open to contemplation and hope.

80. From today onward we commit ourselves—in order to be faithful to this hour of the gospel and of the poor—to a greater intercommunication and mutual help, with greater effectiveness and ecumenical spirit, within the liberating process of the churches of the Third World.

81. All these processes have a global frame of reference. The poor of the Third World are making painful efforts to achieve unity in the common struggle against every kind of colonialism, neocolonialism, and imperialism. The churches must be committed to this effort.

### (e) Conversion and structures of the Church

82. The Church is not invited simply to reform itself, but is rather called to be converted from its personal and structural sins and conformity to the spirit of 'this world' (see Rom. 12:2).

83. If the Church is not converted in its structure, it loses credibility and prophetic power. A rich, dominating church cannot make an option for the world of the poor and oppressed (see Medellín, 'Poverty of the Church'; Puebla, no. 1140).

84. The newness of the Spirit of the risen Christ demands a Church constantly renewed in the service of the new world of the kingdom. In order for the Church to be able to liberate itself and to be a sacramental of liberation, we have to imitate in our Church structures the new way of living together that Jesus inaugurated (see Phil. 2; Matt. 18:15-35; 20:25-28; 23:1-12).

85. In regard to its ministerial structures, this newness obliges the Church to accept as a gift of the Spirit the new ministries that the communities need and are generating. In this new vision, the discrimination that women suffer in the churches cannot be justified biblically, theologically or pastorally.

86. The liberty of the children of God that Jesus teaches with his word, life, and death clearly must also be exercised within the Church itself. This means not passively accepting coercion in the Church, and helping Christian people not to regard as rebelliousness what is intended as free gospel loyalty.

### (f) Specific struggles and global process of liberation

87. The Church of the Third World must commit itself to those struggles for liberation that take up the specific concerns of ethnic, racial, and sex groups, within the overall framework of the struggle of the poor. Indigenous peoples, blacks, and women of the popular classes will always deserve special attention from our Church and a growing concern on the part of our theology.

88. The Church should contribute, from its faith and gospel love, to the end that these various struggles become a genuine joining of forces of oppressed people, without power takeovers that in turn become new modes of oppression. We ought to work together so that this grand alliance and this mutual respect become effective now in the global struggle.

89. As its proper mission, the Church will proclaim and foster in this process those evangelical values that defend the life and liberty of the human person, that open space for communion with the Father and with our brothers and sisters, and that make an original contribution to forging the new person in the new society.

90. The Church, like Jesus, will always be gratuitously present among the weakest and most marginalised, and will always be free and critical before the great and powerful of this world.

### (g) Clarifications

91. The participation of the entire people of God in the inner life of the Christian churches has been continuously growing. The form that this participation has taken in contemporary Church structures has not been an object of our study. But we are happy to see the way our bishops and pastors have on their own initiative taken effective measures to insure that this participation, within the ecclesial community and under their pastoral direction, be ever broader and more effective.

92. The Christian churches, as institutions, should not limit themselves to a particular part of society to the detriment of the universality of Jesus' message. In the

carpenter of Nazareth, God made his option for the poor and oppressed. To be poor is the vocation of the entire Church. But the ecclesial community is open to all—to the rich young man and to Zaccheus—challenging them to respond to the gospel demand to share the poor's aspirations for freedom (Luke 19:1-10).

93. In our societies in the Third World there is a serious division that negates evangelical fraternity by the existence of different social classes. Still, conversion to the gospel of Jesus cannot be limited to becoming aware of the need to be at the side of the oppressed. This is doubtlessly a demand made by the Lord, who sends the rich away empty and fills the hungry with good things. Christian conversion implies, above all, an openness to the Word of Jesus, accepted in faith, lived out in a liberating hope, and made concrete in the love that transforms humankind and the world.

94. We should praise the Lord for Christians' participation in the building of just and fraternal societies. Liberation, its socio-political implications, and the analytical categories that define it are not limited to social theories. Before the social sciences spoke of liberation, the people of God had already achieved it in the Egypt of the Pharaohs. Liberation is at the centre of the biblical message. Within the perspective of our paschal expectations, liberation is not reducible to one or another political model, rather it transcends all history. And it attains its fullness in the manifestation of the kingdom assured by the liberating practice of Jesus and the merciful goodness of the Father.

95. We close our Congress and end this document strengthened by the promise of Jesus to his followers: 'Do not be afraid; I have overcome the world. I am with you always' (John 16:33; Matt. 28:20).

*Note*

1. The term 'popular' has a connotation in English different from the Spanish. In Spanish, it refers to the church comprised of the working class, peasants, and the poor. The expression 'popular Christian communities', as used in this document, carries the same meaning.

# Contributors

PAULO EVARISTO ARNS was born in Brazil in 1921, ordained in 1945, took a doctorate at the Sorbonne in 1952, and was then simultaneously a parish priest in a poor quarter of Rio de Janeiro and professor of patrology and of French for over ten years. In 1966 he was appointed auxiliary bishop of São Paulo, becoming Metropolitan Archbishop of São Paulo in 1970. He was appointed Cardinal by Pope Paul VI in the Consistory of May 1973. The author of thirty books and numerous articles, Cardinal Arns is an authority on early Christian writings, while his pastoral concern has always been for the defence of human rights in the context of the world of work and city slums.

CLODOVIS BOFF was born in Brazil in 1944, and is a priest of the Order of the Servants of Mary. He holds a doctorate in theology from Louvain, and teaches at the Pontifical University of Rio de Janeiro. Besides articles in various reviews, he is the author of four books, including *Teología e Prática* (1978), which has been translated into German, Italian and Spanish, and *Da Libertaçao* (1979).

MARIE-DOMINIQUE CHENU, OP, formerly rector of the Dominican faculties of Le Saulchoir, Paris, formerly professor in the faculty of theology in Paris, has taught the history of theology in the middle ages in its sociological context and then gone on to use the same method in order to gain a pastoral understanding of the contemporary Church. He was a private expert at the Council. His publications include *La Théologie comme science au XIIIe siècle* (Paris 1943); *Introduction à l'étude de St Thomas* (Paris 1950); *Pour une théologie de travail* (Paris 1955); *L'Evangile dans le temps* (Paris 1964); *Peuple de Dieu dans le monde* (Paris 1966); *La Doctrine sociale de l'Eglise comme idéologie* (Brescia 1977).

AGNES CUNNINGHAM gained a doctorate in Sacred Theology (STD) from the Faculties Catholique in Lyons, France. She is professor of patristic theology and early Christianity at Saint Mary of the Lake Seminary, Mundelein, Illinois, in the Archdiocese of Chicago. She is a former president of the Catholic Theological Society of America, and at present vice-president of the Association of Theological Schools of the United States and Canada (1980-82). She is currently on sabbatical in Resistencia, Argentina. She is co-author (with Kosnik *et al*) of *Human Sexuality: New Directions in American Catholic Thought* (1977) and has also written 'Church People as Missionary: A Ministerial Church' (*The Jurist*, 1979: 1/2), and 'Reading the Bible with the Fathers' (*Chicago Studies*, Summer, 1980).

ENRIQUE DUSSEL was born in 1934 in Mendoza, Argentina. He has degrees in philosophy, history and theology. He is at present professor at the Universidad Autonoma de Mexico and in the Department of Religious Sciences in the Universidad Iberamericana. He is also president of the Commission for Studies of the Church in Latin America (CEHILA). He took part in the ecumenical dialogues of Third World theologians in Dar-es-Salaam, Accra, Sri Lanka, São Paulo. His publications include: *Desintegracion de la cristiandad y liberacion* (Salamanca 1978); *Introduccion a la filosofia de la liberacion* (Mexico 1978); *Filosofia de la liberacion* (Mexico 1977): forthcoming English edition: *History of the Church in Latin America* (Grand Rapids 1981); *Ethics and Theology of Liberation* (New York 1978); *Los obispos latinoamerica-*

*nos y la liberacion del pobre* (1504-1620) (Mexico 1979); *De Medellín a Puebla* (Mexico 1979).

DOROTHY FOLLIARD, OP, was born in 1924 and is a Dominican sister of the Adrian, Michigan Congregation. She has a PhD in Latin and Greek (University of Michigan) and degrees in theology and scripture from the University of Chicago Divinity School and Loyola University, Chicago. She is an experienced educator in secondary and college levels. She contributed to position paper, 'The Ordination of Women', sponsored by the US Dominican Leadership Conference, 1978. She is currently teaching in the pastoral institute of the Mexican American Cultural Center, San Antonio, Texas.

KUNO FÜSSEL was born in Trier in 1941. He studied mathematics, physics, philosophy and theology and obtained his doctorate in theology. He is research assistant in Catholic Theology at the University of Münster. He has published on scientific theory, the theory of ideology and the materialist exegesis of the Bible. He is a member of the international movement, Christians for Socialism.

FRANÇOIS HOUTART was born in Belgium in 1925. He holds a doctorate in sociology from the Catholic University of Louvain, where he has been since 1956 a director of the Centre de Recherches Socio-Religieuses and is now professor. He has written numerous works on the sociology of religion, most recently *Eglise et Révolution* (1971, with A. Rousseau); *Religion and Ideology in Sri Lanka* (Hansa 1974) and *Religion et modes de production précapitalistes* (Brussels 1980).

ROBERT MORGAN was born in 1940 in Wales, and studied theology at Cambridge, Durham and Tübingen. He was ordained in the Church of England in 1966 and became lecturer in religious studies at the University of Lancaster in 1967. From 1976 he has been university lecturer in theology and Fellow of Linacre College, Oxford. Among his published works are: *The Nature of New Testament Theology* (1973); ed. (with Michael Pye) *Buddhism and Christianity in Comparative Hermeneutics* (1973); ed. (with Michael Pye) *Ernst Troeltsch: Writings on Theology and Religion* (1977).

JACQUES VAN NIEUWENHOVE was born in Belgium in 1927 and was ordained priest in the White Fathers. He gained a doctorate in theology at the University of Strasburg in 1974. He has taught in the major seminary in Bevundi (1962-67) and also at the International Institute for Catechesis Lumen Vitae. He is at present professor at the University of Nijmegen (Holland) and extraordinary professor at the University of Louvain. He has since 1975 been Secretary to the Conference of Catholic Theological Institutions. He has published articles in such reviews as *Lumen Vitae, Cultures et Developpement, Tijdschrift voor Theologie*.

TSHISHIKU TSHIBANGU has been auxiliary bishop of Kinshasa since 1970. Born at Kipushi, near Lubumbashi, in Zaïre, in 1933, he gained his primary, secondary and university education in his own country before going on to get a doctorate in theology and qualification to teach in a university (agrégation de l'enseignement supérieur) at the University of Louvain, Belgium. He was ordained in 1959. He was made vice-rector of the University of Lovanium, Kinshasa in 1966, rector of the same university in 1967 and has been rector of the National University of Zaïre since 1971. His ecclesiastical offices include his having been an expert at Vatican II between 1963-65, his being a member of the Faith and Order Ecumenical Commission between 1968-77, member of the Roman Secretariat for Non-believers since 1974 and member of the International Theological

Commission between 1969-74. He is also a member of the Editorial Committee of
*Concilium*. His publications include articles on African liturgy and theology as well as
on traditional and contemporary theology and the following books: *Eglise et Nation*.
*L'itinéraire spirituel d'un africain de ce temps* (Kinshasa 1974), *Discours Académiques*
(Kinshasa 1967-76) and *La Théologie comme science au XXème siècle* (Kinshasa 1980).

# CONCILIUM

Claude Geffré. 0 8164 2542 6
144pp.
87. **The Future of Christian
Marriage.** Ed. William Bassett
and Peter Huizing.
0 8164 2575 2.
88. **Polarization in the Church.** Ed.
Hans Küng and Walter Kasper.
0 8164 2572 8 156pp.
89. **Spiritual Revivals.** Ed. Christian
Duquoc and Casiano Floristán.
0 8164 2573 6 156pp.
90. **Power and the Word of God.**
Ed. Franz Bockle and Jacques
Marie Pohier.
0 8164 2574 4 156pp.
91. **The Church as Institution.** Ed.
Gregory Baum and Andrew
Greeley. 0 8164 2575 2 168pp.
92. **Politics and Liturgy.** Ed.
Herman Schmidt and David
Power. 0 8164 2576 0 156pp.
93. **Jesus Christ and Human
Freedom.** Ed. Edward
Schillebeeckx and Bas van
Iersel. 0 8164 2577 9 168pp.
94. **The Experience of Dying.** Ed.
Norbert Greinacher and Alois
Müller. 0 8164 2578 7 156pp.
95. **Theology of Joy.** Ed. Johannes
Baptist Metz and Jean-Pierre
Jossua. 0 8164 2579 5 164pp.
96. **The Mystical and Political
Dimension of the Christian
Faith.** Ed. Claude Geffré and
Gustavo Guttierez.
0 8164 2580 9 168pp.
97. **The Future of the Religious Life.**
Ed. Peter Huizing and William
Bassett. 0 8164 2094 7 96pp.
98. **Christians and Jews.** Ed. Hans
Küng and Walter Kasper.
0 8164 2095 5 96pp.
99. **Experience of the Spirit.** Ed.
Peter Huizing and William
Bassett. 0 8164 2096 3 144pp.
100. **Sexuality in Contemporary
Catholicism.** Ed. Franz Bockle
and Jacques Marie Pohier.
0 8164 2097 1 126pp.
101. **Ethnicity.** Ed. Andrew Greeley
and Gregory Baum.
0 8164 2145 5 120pp.
102. **Liturgy and Cultural Religious
Traditions.** Ed. Herman Schmidt
and David Power. 0 8164 2146 2
120pp.
103. **A Personal God?** Ed. Edward
Schillebeeckx and Bas van
Iersel. 0 8164 2149 8 142pp.
104. **The Poor and the Church.** Ed.
Norbert Greinacher and Alois
Müller. 0 8164 2147 1 128pp.
105. **Christianity and Socialism.** Ed.
Johannes Baptist Metz and
Jean-Pierre Jossua.
0 8164 2148 X 144pp.
106. **The Churches of Africa: Future
Prospects.** Ed. Claude Geffré
and Bertrand Luneau.
0 8164 2150 1 128pp.
107. **Judgement in the Church.** Ed.
William Bassett and Peter
Huizing. 0 8164 2166 8 128pp.
108. **Why Did God Make Me?** Ed.
Hans Küng and Jürgen
Moltmann. 0 8164 2167 6 112pp.

109. **Charisms in the Church.** Ed.
Christian Duquoc and Casiano
Floristán. 0 8164 2168 4 128pp.
110. **Moral Formation and
Christianity.** Ed. Franz Bockle
and Jacques Marie Pohier.
0 8164 2169 2 120pp.
111. **Communication in the Church.**
Ed. Gregory Baum and Andrew
Greeley. 0 8164 2170 6 126pp.
112. **Liturgy and Human Passage.**
Ed. David Power and Luis
Maldonado. 0 8164 2608 2
136pp.
113. **Revelation and Experience.** Ed.
Edward Schillebeeckx and Bas
van Iersel. 0 8164 2609 0 134pp.
114. **Evangelization in the World
Today.** Ed. Norbert Greinacher
and Alois Müller. 0 8164 2610 4
136pp.
115. **Doing Theology in New Places.**
Ed. Jean-Pierre Jossua and
Johannes Baptist Metz.
0 8164 2611 2 120pp.
116. **Buddhism and Christianity.** Ed.
Claude Geffré and Mariasusai
Dhavamony. 0 8164 2612 0
136pp.
117. **The Finances of the Church.** Ed.
William Bassett and Peter
Huizing. 0 8164 2197 8 160pp.
118. **An Ecumenical Confession of
Faith?** Ed. Hans Küng and
Jürgen Moltmann. 0 8164 2198 6
136pp.
119. **Discernment of the Spirit and of
Spirits.** Ed. Casiano Floristán
and Christian Duquoc.
0 8164 2199 4 136pp.
120. **The Death Penalty and Torture.**
Ed. Franz Bockle and Jacques
Marie Pohier. 0 8164 2200 1
136pp.
121. **The Family in Crisis or in
Transition.** Ed. Andrew Greely.
0 567 30001 3 128pp.
122. **Structures of Initiation in Crisis.**
Ed. Luis Maldonado and David
Power. 0 567 30002 1 128pp.
123. **Heaven.** Ed. Bas van Iersel and
Edward Schillebeeckx.
0 567 30003 X 120pp.
124. **The Church and the Rights of
Man.** Ed. Alois Müller and
Norbert Greinacher.
0 567 30004 8 140pp.
125. **Christianity and the Bourgeoisie.**
Ed. Johannes Baptist Metz.
0 567 30005 6 144pp.
126. **China as a Challenge to the
Church.** Ed. Claude Geffré and
Joseph Spae. 0 567 30006 4
136pp.
127. **The Roman Curia and the
Communion of Churches.** Ed.
Peter Huizing and Knut Walf.
0 567 30007 2 144pp.
128. **Conflicts about the Holy Spirit.**
Ed. Hans Küng and Jürgen
Moltmann. 0 567 30008 0 144pp.
129. **Models of Holiness.** Ed.
Christian Duquoc and Casiano
Floristán.
0 567 30009 9 128pp.
130. **The Dignity of the Despised of
the Earth.** Ed. Jacques Marie

Pohier and Dietmar Mieth. 0
567 30010 2 144pp.
131. **Work and Religion.** Ed. Gregory
Baum. 0 567 30011 0 148pp.
132. **Symbol and Art in Worship.** Ed.
Luis Maldonado and David
Power. 0 567 30012 9 136pp.
133. **Right of the Community to a
Priest.** Ed. Edward
Schillebeeckx and Johannes
Baptist Metz. 0 567 30013 7
148pp.
134. **Women in a Men's Church.** Ed.
Virgil Elizondo and Norbert
Greinacher. 0 567 30014 5
144pp.
135. **True and False Universality of
Christianity.** Ed. Claude Geffré
and Jean-Pierre Jossua.
0 567 30015 3 138pp.
136. **What is Religion? An Inquiry for
Christian Theology.** Ed. Mircea
Eliade and David Tracy.
0 567 30016 1 98pp.
137. **Electing our Own Bishops.** Ed.
Peter Huizing and Knut Walf.
0 567 30017 X 112pp.
138. **Conflicting Ways of Interpreting
the Bible.** Ed. Hans Küng and
Jürgen Moltmann. 0 567 30018 8
112pp.
139. **Christian Obedience.** Ed.
Casiano Floristán and Christian
Duquoc. 0 567 30019 6 96pp.
140. **Christian Ethics and Economics:
the North-South Conflict.** Ed.
Dietmar Mieth and Jacques
Marie Pohier. 0 567 30020 X
128pp.

**1981**
141. **Neo-Conservatism: Social and
Religious Phenomenon.** Ed.
Gregory Baum and John
Coleman. 0 567 30021 8.
142. **The Times of Celebration.** Ed.
David Power and Mary Collins.
0 567 30022 6.
143. **God and Father.** Ed. Edward
Schillebeeckx and Johannes
Baptist Metz. 0 567 30023 4.
144. **Tensions Between the Churches
of the First World and the Third
World.** Ed. Virgil Elizondo and
Norbert Greinacher.
0 567 30024 2.
145. **Nietzsche and Christianity.** Ed.
Claude Geffré and Jean-Pierre
Jossua. 0 567 30025 0.
146. **Where Does the Church Stand?**
Ed. Giuseppe Alberigo.
0 567 30026 9.
147. **The Revised Code of Canon
Law: a Missed Opportunity?** Ed.
Peter Huizing and Knut Walf.
0 567 30027 7.
148. **Who Has the Say in the Church?**
Ed. Hans Küng and Jürgen
Moltmann. 0 567 30028 5.
149. **Francis of Assisi: an Example?**
Ed. Casiano Floristán and
Christian Duquoc.
0 567 30029 3.
150. **One Faith, One Church, Many
Moralities?** Ed. Jacques Pohier
and Dietmar Mieth.
0 567 30030 7.

*All back issues are still in print and available for sale. Orders should be
sent to the publishers,*

# T. & T. CLARK LIMITED
# 36 George Street, Edinburgh EH2 2LQ, Scotland